THE MUNITIONETTES

A History of Women's Football in North East England during the Great War

Patrick Brennan

First Published in the UK by Donmouth Publishing
January, 2007

Donmouth Publishing
Riding Lea
Strathmore Road
Rowlands Gill
Tyne & Wear NE39 1JA

ISBN: 978-0-9555063-0-7

Printed and bound by:
Gilpin Press, Pottery Yard, Houghton-le-Spring,
Tyne & Wear DH4 4BA
Tel: (0191) 584 2267

Preface

Until recent years the very existence of the Munition Girls football teams of World War 1 was a well-kept secret. Thanks however to two excellent books by Gail Newsham and Barbara Jacobs, the exploits of the Dick, Kerr Ladies of Preston have become known to a wider audience. But although the achievements of the Dick, Kerr team should not be underestimated, they were not the first in the field, and theirs was not the full story. The present work is an attempt to redress the balance, and to tell the story of the Munition Girl Footballers of north east England during those dark and far-off days.

It is a story which should have been commenced several years ago, when many of the ladies who feature in it were still alive. In common with most of their generation, they said little about their wartime exploits, and although their descendants knew that Mum had played football as a girl, they were told very little else. The tale has, therefore, been put together largely from contemporary newspaper reports. It reveals a world of contrasts; the youthful enthusiasm of the young women footballers, who stepped beyond the bounds of social conventions to raise money for charity, set against the awful reality of the most disastrous human conflict in history.

I should like to thank the following descendants of Munitionettes who responded to my letters in the local press and kindly shared their memories with me – Yvonne Crawford, John Morgan, Sheila Angus, Peter McNaughton, Olive and Martin Carrott, Winnie Brass and Ken Pratt.

I should also like to thank the staff of the Public Library services in the North East who were so helpful to me in my research, and who responded patiently to my requests for volume after volume of newspaper archives. In this regard, special posthumous thanks go to Tom Marshall, formerly librarian at Gateshead Central Library. Tom, whose own mother played in goal for a women's football team, researched this subject during the 1980's. It appears to have been his intention to publish a book, but sadly he died before this could be accomplished. His archive of clippings, photographs, articles and handwritten manuscripts is preserved by Gateshead Central Library, and it provided a very useful starting point for some of my enquiries.

The front cover shows Emma Hicks,
a member of the Morpeth Post Office Girls FC, 1917

(Photograph courtesy of Virginia Blakey)

Contents

Page

1. The Girls take the field 1
2. The Munitionettes' Cup 1917-18 14
3. Munitionette Internationals 25
4. County and District Matches 31
5. The Munitionettes' Cup 1918-19 41
6. Postscript 48
7. Sources and references 54
8. Appendix 1 - Tabulated match results 1916-19 55
9. Appendix 2 - An alphabetical list of players 102
10. Appendix 3 –North East Munitions companies 117

Chapter 1
The Girls take the field

"We made munitions during the day and devoted our spare time to football. We had a large following"

In this brief, matter-of-fact way, Bella Grey (nee Metcalfe), formerly the captain of Blyth Spartans Munitions Ladies F.C., summed up one of the most fascinating social phenomena of the Great War - the emergence of the Munition Girls football teams.

When, in 1914, the country's young men marched off to war in an excess of patriotic fervour, the womenfolk of Britain also felt the need to do something for the cause. Initially, this involved upper and middle-class ladies engaging in various kinds of voluntary work through organisations such as Voluntary Aid Detachments (VAD), the management of which was in the hands of the Red Cross and the St John's Ambulance Associations. The number of working-class women employed actually fell during the early months of the war owing to a decline in demand in the millinery and textile trades. However, two factors were about to change this, and together they would result in a dramatic increase in the number of women employed in heavy industry.

Firstly, the war was not "all over by Christmas", as many volunteers expected. On all fronts an initial campaign of territorial incursions rapidly became bogged down in the stalemate of trench warfare. As the military campaign continued to soak up both human and material resources, it became clear to the Government that women would be needed in large numbers for factory work. This was not a popular move; working men objected to women taking over their jobs, and formulated all sorts of spurious reasons as to why they were not capable of doing so. They were caught in a cleft stick; they did not accept that women should be paid the same as men, but at the same time were anxious that the entry of women into the workplace might result in a general lowering of wages. In consequence, talks with the Trades Unions on "Dilution" – the employment of unskilled men and women on jobs previously reserved for skilled men, had made very little progress when the Liberal Government was brought down by the great "Shell Scandal" of May 1915. This was the revelation by Colonel Repington, the Military Correspondent of The Times, that the troops at the Front were being hampered by a shortage of munitions. In describing a failed attack upon German positions around Fromelles and Richebourg he wrote, "the want of an unlimited supply of high explosive was a fatal bar to our success." Fatal indeed – after a wholly ineffective shrapnel barrage against solid trench parapets, several feet thick, the British infantry had bravely charged the German trenches only to encounter withering fire from the enemy machine guns. There was a public outcry, and in response the Government created the Ministry of Munitions, to take the manufacture of munitions directly under its control. With Lloyd George at its head this new Ministry pushed through changes to industrial practices which had served as a barrier to women's employment, and, with the assistance of Mrs Emmeline Pankhurst, it actively encouraged the recruitment of women into the munitions factories.

Secondly, by the end of 1916 the opposing sides had fought themselves to a standstill. The disastrous Somme offensive had resulted in 420,000 British casualties, and despite the introduction of conscription the army was running out of men. Women were urged to move even further into traditionally male roles, in order to release more men for the front. The North East of England, with a huge concentration of industry manufacturing ships, armaments and other materials for the war effort, was one area in which the recruitment of women was particularly important.

The largest manufacturer of armaments and other military equipment in the region was the firm of Sir W.G. Armstrong, Whitworth & Co. This company's facilities at Scotswood, Elswick, Walker, Gateshead, Birtley, and Gosforth produced a vast array of war matériel, including shells, naval guns, machine guns, ships and aeroplanes. Traditional arms manufacturers could not, however, keep up with demand; this was the first war in history to be fought by economies as much as by armies, and following the establishment of the Ministry of Munitions virtually the whole industrial output of Great Britain was diverted to the war effort. (In 1917, military spending in the UK reached 70% of Gross National Product)

Shipyards, steelworks, rope and cable manufacturers, glass manufacturers, chemical plants, textile manufacturers - all were designated as munitions factories if they held a contract from the Ministry of Munitions, and many went further and converted part of their premises into shell manufacturing shops. Even companies used to making mundane items such as bicycles, sewing-machines, lawn mowers and such like now found themselves making shells, or components of shells. (The actual filling of the shells with explosive was generally done elsewhere, for reasons of safety, not of the employees, but of the manufacturing facilities themselves.)

The employees of such works were subject to restrictions on their movement, and could be fined by a "Munitions Tribunal" for a whole range of minor offences, such as reporting late for a shift. In addition to ensuring a high attendance rate, the establishment was also concerned about the moral welfare of the young women employed in the munitions factories. Female Supervisors, who acted as Welfare Officers, watched over them at work, and they were backed up by the Women's Police Service, whose tasks included carrying out searches of female employees, and dealing with drunkenness and "immorality" away from the workbench.

Many young working-class women responded enthusiastically to the call, not just for reasons of patriotism, but also to break free from the domestic drudgery that was their only other hope of gainful employment. The reaction of society in general was at first somewhat patronising; a popular song of the day, "The Munition Workers' Song," sung by Robert Radford, contains the refrain:

So we are at the benches, and our pals are in the trenches,
And all our work serves the end,
And mere women too, are here to help us through,
In our efforts our world to defend

In fact, these "mere women" performed almost every available task that their male counterparts had previously done, and would eventually comprise a majority of the workforce.

Never before had such a large cohort of young females found themselves thrown together so closely. They enjoyed their new-found freedom, even though they were working in dangerous conditions, with rates of pay approximately half that of their male co-workers. They organised social activities among themselves, and one of the recreational outlets they explored was football.

Strictly speaking, women's football was not entirely new. The North-East had witnessed it before. In 1895, and again in 1896, Miss Nettie Honeyball and her "British Ladies' Football Club" visited the region during their tours of Britain, and staged at least five exhibition matches - at Jesmond and St James's Park in Newcastle, two matches at Mowbray Road in South Shields and one at Feethams in Darlington. The match at St. James's Park, played on 20th April 1895, attracted a crowd of 8,000, a record for the time. It was a passing fancy though; this first attempt at establishing an organisational structure for women's football was essentially a middle-class venture, and middle-class women were not yet united in favour of the struggle for female rights. Even the feminists among them would probably have baulked at taking the field themselves, though they would certainly have given moral support to the footballers. Despite occasional efforts on the part of some pioneers, such as the ladies of Wheatley Hill who in 1909 formed the Rosy Rapids A.F.C., the women's game failed to take root in the region.

The Football Association for its part did nothing to assist or encourage women's football. In 1902 they passed a resolution banning mixed-sex competitive matches - a ban which is still in force if you happen to be over 11 years of age.

The upheaval which accompanied the Great War overturned turned many existing social conventions, and women's football experienced a revival, as teams sprang up in munitions factories all over the country. It is not difficult to understand why this was so; a casual game of football can be played under almost any conditions, and with any number of participants. Organising a lunch-time kickabout requires no more than a couple of coats to act as goalposts, and something roughly approximating to a ball. Young male employees in the war-time factories would certainly have played in their spare moments, and their female counterparts may have been drawn in to the action.

The transition from casual knockabouts to organised games came about when it was realised that women's football had entertainment potential, which might be put to use in raising funds for the many war-related charities in existence. League football had ceased at the end of the 1914-15 season, and several of the local minor leagues had also shut down for the duration of the war. Those which continued were under strict instructions from the F.A. that players should not be paid, and that cups, medals and other such trophies should not be awarded. Consequently the fare that was being offered to the spectators was mediocre. In these circumstances, the prospect of watching two teams of women battle it out on the field proved irresistible for many, especially when coupled with the knowledge that the proceeds of the games would go to good causes. This also made the game more respectable - even Harrods had a ladies football team.

In the North East the first organised game between women munition workers to be reported in the newspapers took place at Wallsend on 3rd February 1917, when the Wallsend Slipway & Engineering Company played the North East Marine Engineering Company to raise funds for the Queen Mary Needlework Guild. The game was played at the Wallsend F.C. ground, and was kicked off by Mrs. Roland Hodge, the wife of the Managing Director of the Northumberland Shipbuilding Company. The match was refereed by Bill McCracken, the Newcastle United and Northern Ireland full-back, and before the game and during the interval the Jarrow Navvies' Band played to entertain the crowd, which numbered about 2,000. The team from North East Marine won the game 3-0.

Wallsend Slipway and North East Marine - the pioneers of women's football in the North-East according to the Northern Echo, were to play against each other regularly over the next two years, though they did also compete against other sides.

The game got going in the south of the region not long afterwards. The first match played at Hartlepool took place at the Victoria Ground on Easter Monday, 7th April 1917, between teams of munition girls from the Central Marine Engine Works and the Expanded Metal Company, better known locally as the "Expansion". The crowd of 4-5,000 was the largest seen at the ground since the commencement of the war, so great was the interest in this strange new spectacle, and at an entry price of 6d the takings in aid of Yorkshire Prisoners of War would have been in the region of £100. The account of the game in the Northern Daily Mail makes interesting reading; the reporter seemed surprised by the fact that "the girls wore distinguishing colours - just the same as in ordinary football". The players "seemed to know little of the rudiments of the game, but plodded on from end to end, causing endless amounts of fun and excitement." The Expanded Metal Company won by a single goal scored by Lizzie Kane.

This set the pattern for these games - the women's teams did not play in organised leagues, but met in friendly matches for charitable causes. The games were invariably kicked off by a local celebrity, and a band would be in attendance. Initially the Press did not know how to refer to them - "Female Munitions Workers", "Munitions Ladies", "Munitions Girls" and "Fair Footballers" were some of the titles they were given. In the following season they would come to be known generally as "Munitionettes".

Both local and national charities benefited from the matches. At a local level the beneficiary most frequently encountered was the local Welcome Home or Heroes' Fund, which provided support to soldiers and sailors who had "Copped a Blighty", – i.e. had been invalided home. In some towns a Mayor's Charity existed, which presumably covered a wide range of deserving causes. Aged Miners' Homes and local hospitals also figured largely in the list of beneficiaries. An important Newcastle charity was the Joseph and Jane Cowen Home for the Retraining of Wounded Soldiers and Sailors. This was located at Benwell Grange, and was established thanks to the generosity of Miss Cowen of Stella Hall in memory of her mother and her father, a prominent local politician and businessman.

At the national level there were many charities. Some were general in nature, such as The Comrades of the Great War, founded in 1917 as a non-political and democratic organisation to foster comradeship and mutual help. Others had specific objectives, such as "Jack's Bairns", sometimes referred to as "Jack and Tom's Bairns" (the Jack being Jack Tar - i.e. a sailor, and the Tom being Tommy Atkins, the name by which British soldiers were collectively known). This charity provided for the welfare of war orphans. The Jack Cornwell Cottage Homes for Disabled Sailors was a charity named after John Travers Cornwell, the boy V.C., who lost his life at the Battle of Jutland. The London-based St Dunstan's Hospital for Blinded Soldiers and Sailors was founded in 1915, and still exists today. The Queen Mary's Needlework Guild hardly sounds like a war charity, but it was instituted to make and distribute items of warm clothing for the men in the trenches. As might be expected the Red Cross, Dr. Barnardo's Homes, the Y.M.C.A. and Y.W.C.A. also figured quite frequently. One charity which few today would have heard of, but which attracted quite a lot of support, was the Haverfield Fund for the Serbian Red Cross. This was named after Evelina Haverfield, who before the war was an active suffragette, and who spent most of its duration in the Balkans commanding an ambulance corps in support of the Serbian Army.

The Munitionettes generally wore normal football jerseys, but their lower body clothing underwent a process of evolution. Some of the earlier team photographs show them in full-length trousers, or knee-length skirts, but as munitionette football became more serious they started to wear 'knickers'. Lest there be any doubt, this was the term used at the time to describe men's football shorts. One aspect of their garb which did not change however was the headgear; they wore mobcaps in team colours, a practical measure given the hair styles of the day.

Tyneside had the largest concentration of teams, mostly based on the heavy industries along the riverside. Armstrong, Whitworth and Co. had no fewer than 9 teams from their various premises, while other prominent employers who were represented included Palmers, Hood Haggies, North East Marine Engineering, Wallsend Slipway and Engineering, Angus Sanderson, Foster, Blackett and Wilson, and the Newcastle upon Tyne Motor Company.

On Teesside, Dorman Long and Co. had three teams, representing their Britannia, Warrenby and Port Clarence sites respectively. There were also two teams from Richardson Westgarth's Teesside site, and one each from Smith's Dock and Bolckow, Vaughan & Co. Further up the river, Darlington was represented by Rise Carr, Railway Athletic and Robert Stephenson & Co. The town of Stockton did not join in until 1918, when a team was formed at Ashmore, Benson, Pease & Co.

There were four main teams at Hartlepool, based at the Central Marine Engine Works, the Expanded Metal Company, Brown's Sawmills and Richardson, Westgarth & Company. Belle Vue Munition Girls and Shipyard United also made brief appearances.

Sunderland had three main teams - Glaholm, Robson & Co., Webster & Co., and Sunderland Ladies. The latter was not associated with a particular employer, but was formed as a result of an advertisement placed in the Sunderland Daily Echo on 29th September 1917. The objective of the team was to raise funds for Sunderland Hospitals, and ladies wishing to play were invited to apply to Mr George Lepine, 39 Stobart Street, Monkwearmouth. Attempts were made to form a Wearside Ladies AFC, and a team representing Robert Thompson and Co., but these do not appear to have got off the ground.

Given the women's lack of experience in competitive football it is not surprising that these initial ventures caused some merriment amongst the spectators. It also led to some interesting new tactics being displayed on occasions. When North East Marine played Swan Hunter's on 10th March 1917 their stronger and more experienced team were cruising to a 4-0 win with minutes to go when, as the Northern Echo reported, "the shipyard girls formed themselves into a bunch and rushed the ball into the net, Mason giving it the final touch. A similar rush was rewarded with a penalty, from which Elvin scored."

Palmer's of Jarrow had only three practice matches before their first competitive game, against Armstrong's Naval Yard on 12th May 1917. Despite their relatively recent introduction to the game, and the intimidating effect of playing in front of 2,000 spectators, they acquitted themselves well against their more experienced opponents, losing by only 2-0 to goals from Ina Wardaugh and Bella Thompson. The game raised £75 6s. 6d. for charity.

The reaction of the football authorities in the area was initially encouraging. When the Durham County F.A. held its Annual General Meeting on 26th May 1917, the secretary, Mr. W. Spedding, hit back at those critics who were still calling for football to be banned altogether for the duration of the war. He pointed to the example of the lady munition workers. Though the ladies' clubs were not affiliated with the county associations "their enthusiasm was stimulating, and was assisting the others to bear with fortitude their own burdens." He extended best wishes to the female workers and "hoped that their charitable efforts would be crowned with success."

Because their matches were organised in aid of charity, the teams sometimes found themselves travelling a fair distance to perform. As an example, on 14th July 1917 Palmer's met Wallsend Slipway at Croft Park, Blyth, in aid of the Blyth Military Merit and Homecoming Funds. Slipway proved too strong for Palmer's, winning 4-0 on the day.

The distances they travelled in order to play were not only physical; on 6th August 1917 Wallsend Slipway and North East Marine were engaged to play an "exhibition football match" for a Bank Holiday fete held at "The Ridings", Hexham. Compared to the rough streets of Wallsend, the genteel atmosphere of this Hexhamshire country home would have seemed like a different planet. The game, refereed by Bill McCracken, ended in a 1-1 draw, and afterwards the ball, signed by all the players, was auctioned, raising a further £2 for charity.

Sometimes the games were not altogether serious affairs. On 21st July 1917 the women of Armstrong's No. 60 Shop (Elswick) took on Ryton Girls at Prudhoe in what was described as a "Novelty Costume football match" in aid of the Prudhoe and District Welcome Home Fund.

On occasions the organisers would match a team of men against the women, in order to add an extra degree of interest (and hopefully swell the gate receipts). The first recorded game of this nature in the North East actually pre-dates the all-women matches; it took place on Boxing Day, 1916, at Hebburn Argyle's ground, and involved teams of male and female munition workers from Hawthorn, Leslie and Co.'s shipyard. The women won by 6 goals to 2, but it was not a serious affair, the men playing in "comic costumes," according to the Daily Chronicle. Somewhat surprisingly, in view of their emphatic victory, the Hawthorn Leslie's women's team played no further part in munitionette football after this date.

When they were not hampered by fancy dress it was common for the men to play with their hands tied behind their backs, apart from the goalkeeper, who was allowed to have one hand free. Several such matches took place in the North East; for example on 18th August 1917 the munition girls of Brown's Mills, West Hartlepool were defeated 2-1 by a Military XI at the Victoria ground. On 6th October 1917 the Darlington N.E.R. munition girls played a team of wounded soldiers from the Woodside Hospital in aid of the Soldiers' Comforts Fund. The game took place at Feethams, the home of Darlington F.C. and resulted in a win for the Soldiers by 7 goals to 6.

A more bizarre example of handicapping was a match which took place at Stanley on 24th November 1917. A team of munitionettes from Armstrong-Whitworth's No 43 Shop (Elswick) faced a side of ex-soldiers from the Joseph and Jane Cowen Rehabilitation Home at Benwell. To add novelty value the organisers fielded a team comprising eight one-legged and two one-armed men (one assumes the goalkeeper was not an amputee). The final score was 6-4 in favour of the "Wounded Warriors", who were assisted by the award of two penalties. Although the event undoubtedly raised much-needed funds for local charities, it is hard not to feel that the women were being subject to a certain amount of exploitation on this occasion.

Munitionette encounters were not confined to the normal football season, but continued during the summer months. It was fairly predictable therefore that someone would suggest a women's cricket match. Such an event was organised by the Darlington Railway Athletic Club at the Brinkburn Ground, Darlington, on 28th July 1917. Teams representing the Cartridge Case and 18-inch Shell Shops respectively battled it out, the Cartridge Case Shop winning by 68 runs to 30. Their bowling skills were evidently higher than their batting skills, as the top bowlers for each side, Miss Elliott and Miss Bell, took 7 wickets for 7 runs and 5 wickets for 7 runs respectively. Another cricket match, this time between a team of women and soldiers from a Training Reserve Battalion, took place at Birtley Cricket Ground on 18th August 1917. The women, batting first, scored 138 runs, and the men, handicapped by having to bat left-handed, replied with 160 runs. This match was in aid of the Cowen Training Home for Disabled Soldiers and Sailors in Newcastle. The Birtley ladies played a further match a month later, this time against Sacriston Ambulance Brigade in aid of the "Sacriston" bed at the V.A.D. hospital in France. Their run-getting was not so good on this occasion; the innings closed at 64 all out, and in response the men scored 68 for nine wickets, six of which were run-outs, suggesting they were not taking things too seriously.

The munitionettes generally played under the names of the companies they worked for, but one notable exception was a team which was to become the strongest in the area - Blyth Spartans Ladies' FC. This team was formed by a group of young women working in the South Docks area of Blyth. Their job was loading ships with ammunition for the front, and unloading cargoes of used shell cases for recycling. In their spare time they played football on the sands, watched by admiring sailors, and following the visit of Palmers and Wallsend Slipway on 14th July 1917 they realised that they were good enough to compete at this level. With assistance and some coaching from their naval friends they formed a team, and on 4th August 1917 they played their first public game against their mentors at Croft Park, the home of North-Eastern leaguers Blyth Spartans, who had ceased operations at the end of the 1914-15 season. The women defeated the

"Jack Tars" 7-2, and the proceeds of the game went to support the relatives of those recently killed on H.M.S. Vaughan. Blyth Spartans donated a set of their famous green and white striped jerseys to the women, who adopted the club name, and on 20th August 1917 they took the field as Blyth Spartans Munitions Ladies against another local team, the Blyth United Munition Ladies. This game was also played at Croft Park, in aid of the Cowpen and Crofton Workmen's Patriotic Fund. In common with most of the munitionette games it had the air of a cup-tie, with a band performing prior to the match, and a local jeweller, Herron's, donated souvenir brooches to be presented to the members of both sides. The game was kicked off formally by Mrs. Rowell, and then, as the match report states, "Play was rather one-sided, the Spartans almost from the beginning being on the aggressive. They scored ten goals while the United registered one." The Spartans team included several names who were to become well-known both within and outside the region, in particular their centre-forward, 17-year-old Bella Reay.

Not everyone in Blyth was pleased with this development, and tongues evidently started to wag. This prompted a letter to the Blyth News which was published on 30th August 1917. The author – "Munitioneer", did not mince his words in defence of the newly-formed teams:

> *I have heard, more than once, some very uncharitable and uncalled-for criticism of the respectability of the young women playing these matches, certain of the "unco guid" asserting that it is not decent for them to appear in public in "knickers!" - pardon my mentioning the article of clothing that has raised their ire.*
>
> *May I say that these girls are doing an excellent work of charity in playing. We cannot all subscribe hard cash to the hundred and one deserving funds now calling for our support. They are doing their bit by work; all honour to them.*
>
> *I should like to suggest that they are more decently dressed in the "unmentionable" garments than their prurient minded critics who are parading the streets in blouses open nearly to the waist and skirts too short for a girl of 12. I am working with these girls and I am proud of it. Some of them are a bit boisterous, but they all have hearts as big as a lion. If some of the weak-minded and weak-kneed could only have seen them stick in manfully during the recent inclement weather they would feel reassured that there is no possible doubt of our winning the war while we have such women (heroines I call them) as mothers of the race.*
>
> MUNITIONEER

It is fairly clear from this letter that the "uncalled-for criticism" was coming from other women.

Blyth Spartans were also the only team to venture outside the region. On 20th April 1918 they journeyed to Brunton Park, Carlisle, to take on the Carlisle Munition Girls in a game to raise funds for the Carlisle Citizen's League for Borders Prisoners of War. Jennie Morgan opened the scoring for Blyth with a deceptive shot across the goal, and Bella Reay netted a further two in Blyth's 3-0 win. An even more emphatic 5-0 win for Blyth was the result in the return match at Croft Park on 1st June.

Given the relative proximity of Carlisle and its environs it is surprising that more contests between North-East and Cumbrian teams did not take place. Women's football in Cumbria had started somewhat later, but once underway the participants were soon demonstrating the same degree of keenness and enthusiasm as their sisters on Tyneside and Teesside. Teams from Whitehaven and Workington appear to have been the pioneers in this region; their first encounter took place on 5th May 1917 at Whitehaven cricket field, to raise funds for the new Military Hospital at Moresby House. A crowd of 5,000, including several hundred who had travelled from Workington, watched the game, which was keenly contested. Whitehaven held the visitors to a goalless draw, thanks in no small measure to an excellent performance by their goalkeeper, Kitty Cowie.

Compared to the North-East however, the geographical and industrial circumstances of Cumbria were not quite as favourable for the development of munitionette football. There was not the same great concentration of industry, the munitions companies generally being smaller and more widely dispersed. In addition to Whitehaven and Workington, the coastal towns of Maryport, Seaton and Harrington, and inland centres of Carlisle, Cockermouth and Cleator had munitions works. Some of these manufactured shells, for example Pratchitt's engineering works in Carlisle, while others, such as at Cockermouth and Cleator, were involved in the production of textiles. In the case of Derwent Mills at Cockermouth, the main product was high quality linen cloth for covering aircraft wings, while the mills at Cleator mainly produced military uniforms. Strangely, although the largest munitions works on the planet was situated a few miles north of Carlisle, at Gretna, the women employees there took very little part in organised football, although the ammunition depot at Mossband, through which a lot of Gretna's output passed, did possess an active team. The Cumbrian teams which did exist played regularly against each other, and in aid of the same charitable causes as those in the North-East. It seems however that the extra distance was just too great, either in terms of expense, or time, to justify regular contact between the two regions.

A departure from the normal match format took place on 1st September 1917 at the Friarage Ground, Hartlepool, when 10 teams representing five local companies took part in a six-a-side tournament organised for the benefit of the Missions to Seamen. There was a good turnout of 1,500 spectators, despite the unfavourable weather, which saw the final stages of the tournament take place in pouring rain. The games were contested on the basis of goals and minors, a "minor" being scored when the ball passed between a goalpost and a flag placed in the ground a few yards from it. The winner of the tournament was the Brown's No. 1 team who defeated the Central Marine Engine Works in the final by 3 minors to nil. Matilda Booth, a promising member of the Brown's team, returned home to find her father Joseph, a Welsh rugby international, absolutely livid at the thought of his daughter playing football in public. He forbade her from playing again, but his daughter was evidently of an independent mind as she was still playing for Brown's in 1919.

Munitionette teams were, by their very nature, working-class, and women of a higher social standing did not normally become involved at the physical level, though some may have helped out with organisational matters. A rare exception to this rule was a match which took place on 23rd February 1918, in which the ladies of Armstrong College, the forerunner of Newcastle University, played against Chester-le-Street Ladies. The result, a 7-1 win for Armstrong College, seems to have satisfied their curiosity, as there is no record of them having ventured onto the field again.

Some of the teams which formed endured for a considerable time, while others made only a brief appearance in the record. An example of the latter was the Blyth United Munition Ladies. After their 10-0 drubbing at the hands of Blyth Spartans they never again played another women's team, confining their activities to matches against men, where the football took second priority to the pantomime element of the entertainment. Another side which lasted only a short while was the Belle Vue munition ladies of West Hartlepool, who first appeared on the scene at Seaham Hall on 13th October 1917 in a match against Brown's Munitionettes, and played only two more games, in each case against the same opponents. In this case however the Belle Vue side may have been a pseudonym for Brown's second XI, as the names of several of their players crop up in the Brown's first team on other occasions.

Other sides which appear in the record seem to have been only scratch sides, got together for perhaps only a few games, or even a single event. Sacriston Ladies, Houghton Ladies, Burradon Ladies, Morpeth Post Office Girls and Trimdon Grange Ladies possibly fall into this category.

As the women built up more playing experience some real stars emerged, and the Press began to acknowledge their genuine abilities. On 13th October 1917 the Middlesbrough Herald noted, "Female teams are springing up rapidly, and show they can play a 'gentlemanly' game. Shall we see mixed teams before the close of the season?"

Certainly their enthusiasm for the game knew no bounds. A good example is the case of Jennie Nuttall, Blyth Spartans' regular left-winger. On 13th October 1917 she featured in the Spartans side which played Burradon Ladies in aid of the Soldiers' and Sailors' Comforts Fund. Jennie got two goals in Spartans' 4-1 win, but had more than this feat to celebrate; she had been married that very morning at St Cuthbert's, Blyth, and had hurried from the church to take part in the game!

Another dedicated player was Sarah Cornforth of Birtley. She married in 1912, and had a small child. With her husband away fighting in France she had a difficult time making ends meet, but she loved her football, and played under her maiden name of Sally Matthews until December 1917. By then, her prowess on the field, in particular her penalty-kicking ability, had reached a level at which she no longer needed to worry about clucking tongues of disapproval.

Chapter 2

The Munitionettes' Cup 1917-18

As the number and popularity of Munitionettes' games began to increase, efforts were made to improve the organisational structures. One such effort took place in Hartlepool, where representatives from five teams - Richardson Westgarth, Expansion, Brown's Athletic Club, Shipyard United and Central Marine Engine Works got together on 5th September 1917 under the chairmanship of Councillor Harry Salmon to discuss forming a Munitionettes' League. They decided to go ahead, but their enthusiasm seems to have waned later, and this interesting suggestion does not appear to have been taken any further.

More success was achieved in organising a knock-out tournament. On 20th August 1917 the Daily Chronicle carried an article entitled "Munition Girls' Challenge Cup". A solid silver trophy had been donated for a knock-out competition to be held between Munition Girls. The competition would be organised along the following lines; charitable organisations would apply for cup-ties to be allocated to them, and they would be expected to make all the necessary arrangements. The teams would turn up on the day and play, and whatever takings were made at the gate would go to charity. It was envisaged that charities such as Soldiers' Welcome Home Funds, Prisoner of War Funds, Aged Miners' Homes, Soldiers' and Sailors' Orphans Funds and such like would be supported in this way.

The term "Munition Girls" was to be interpreted rather widely; "Ladies' teams from Tyneside District drawn from any establishment or concern such as works, factories, mills, railways, tramways, collieries, shops etc. will be allowed to compete".

The article did not reveal the donor of the trophy, but its official title was the "Tyne Wear & Tees Alfred Wood Munition Girls Cup", suggesting that it may have been given in memory of Alfred Wood, a partner in the Hartley-Wood Glass Company of Sunderland, who died in 1916.

The response from eligible teams was encouraging; Armstrongs Naval Yard, Birtley Cartridge Case Factory and Blyth Spartans were among the first to express an interest, and they were quickly followed by further teams from the Armstrong-Whitworth organisation (43, 50, 53 and 57 Shops), as well as Wallsend Slipway, North East Marine Engineering (Wallsend), Angus-Sanderson (Gateshead), Swan Hunter (Wallsend), South Benwell N.U.T.,

Irvine's (Hartlepool), Bolckow-Vaughan (Middlesbrough and Cambois), Brown's (Hartlepool), Expansion (Hartlepool), Richardson Westgarth (Hartlepool), Dorman Long, Trimdon Grange, Blyth United and Palmer's (Jarrow and Hebburn). The organising committee held a meeting at Shields Cafe in the Bigg Market, Newcastle, on September 8th, at which the trophy was on display, and the final touches were made to the organisation of the tournament. Applications were invited from qualified referees, a preference being expressed for discharged soldiers.

It was decided at an early stage to split the competition along regional lines, with separate sections for Tyneside/Wearside and for Teesside. Not all the expressions of interest were converted into formal entries, but by 21st September 14 teams had signed up for the Northern section, and the organisers were hoping for a further 2 to complete the draw. In the event these did not materialise, and when the draw for the first round was made on 26th September 1917 two teams received a bye. The full draw was as follows:

Armstrong's Naval Yard v Angus Sanderson
Armstrong-Whitworth 57 Shop v Armstrong-Whitworth 43 Shop
Wallsend Slipway v Armstrong-Whitworth 60 Shop
South Benwell Motor Works v North East Marine
Birtley Cartridge Case Factory v Palmer's Jarrow
Blyth United v Aviation Athletic
Armstrong-Whitworth 40 Shop and R. H. Hood Haggie's (byes)

Somewhat surprisingly none of the Hartlepools teams entered the Teesside section, which received a total of 12 entries. The draw for this section took place at Buck's Clifton Temperance Hotel, Middlesbrough, on 6th October. Both the first and second rounds were drawn at the same meeting, as follows:

Round 1

A - Dorman, Long (Port Clarence) v Bolckow, Vaughan
B - Dorman No. 1 Shell Shop v Richardson, Westgarth No. 1
C - T.D. Ridley's (Skinningrove) v Skinningrove Iron Works
D - Darlington Railway Athletic v Darlington Rise Carr

Smith's Dock, Richardson-Westgarth No. 2, Dorman, Long No. 2 and Stephenson's (Darlington) received byes

Round 2

Smith's Dock v Dorman Long No 2
Winner of A v Winner of C
Winner of D v Richardson, Westgarth No. 2
Winner of B v Stephenson's Works

The first ties in the competition were played on Saturday October 13th. In the Northern section 57 Shop met 43 Shop at Blaydon Road, Scotswood, the home of Scotswood FC. 57 Shop kicked off, and quickly scored through Ethel Wallace. 43 Shop lacked experience (this was, in fact, their first competitive game), but showed lots of spirit, and eventually equalised with a goal from M. Dryden. 57 Shop proved too strong, however, and Ella Fairbairn put them further ahead before half time. In the second half play was more evenly balanced, but 57 Shop gained a penalty, which Ethel Wallace converted to make the final score 3-1 in their favour. The proceeds of this game were donated to the Scotswood Welcome Home and Heroes' Recognition Funds.

The Teesside section commenced on the same day, with a meeting between Bolckow, Vaughan & Co. and Dorman, Long & Co. (Port Clarence), at Ayresome Park. The game was kicked off formally by the Mayoress, Mrs Joseph Calvert, and resulted in a 1-1 draw. Proceeds in this case were for the Middlesbrough War Heroes' Fund.

Although only one tie had been played in the Northern section, the committee nevertheless went ahead and made the draw for the second round on 19th October. This brought in the teams which had received a bye in the first round. The result of the draw was as follows:

Wallsend Slipway or 60 Shop v 40 Shop
NEM or NUT v Blyth or Aviation
Sandersons or Naval Yard v Hood Haggie's
57 Shop v Birtley or Palmer's

The organisers were already beginning to experience some frustration in their attempts to keep the competition moving forward. The match between Blyth and Aviation which was scheduled to take place at New Hartley on 20th October had to be postponed, as the Sporting Man bluntly commented, "owing to the military authorities refusing to allow the game to proceed, although expense has been incurred." This was probably due to the local military commander deciding he wanted to use the ground on the day. At the commencement of the war many football grounds had been commandeered by the Army, as they were ideal for practising field gun drills and other such exercises. (It was not only small, non-League grounds which were affected - part of Newcastle United's pitch was lifted in April 1915 to create space for temporary offices for the War Ministry Accounts Department, and the main stand at Tottenham Hotspur's ground was converted into a gas-mask factory for the duration of the war.)

The progress of the competition received a boost the following Saturday when a total of four ties were played, though not all of them were decided. In the first of these, Palmer's and Birtley Cartridge Case Factory travelled to Bishop Auckland to raise money for the flag day of the Sailors' Orphans' Home Scheme, otherwise known as "Jack's Bairns Day". A good crowd was in attendance, and the game was well contested by the two teams. Despite numerous exciting incidents however, neither side managed to score, and a 0-0 draw was the final result.

There was more excitement at Blaydon Road, where Armstrong Whitworth's 60 Shop took on Wallsend Slipway. This was effectively a home match for the 60 Shop girls, and they took full advantage of it. The match kicked off in wretched conditions, and 60 Shop managed to bottle up their opponents in their own territory for much of the first half, but seemed incapable of making a breakthrough. Fate lent them a hand shortly before the interval when Slipway conceded a penalty, which the 60 Shop centre-forward Bella Willis put away without difficulty. A few minutes later the same player found the net again to make the half-time score 2-0, and this proved to be the final result.

The tie between N.U.T. Motor Works and North East Marine was also played to a conclusion. The match took place at Hawkey's Lane, North Shields, the pre-war home of North Shields Athletic, in aid of the widow and family of the late Secretary of North Shields YMCA. There was a good crowd for the game, which North East Marine won 3-0, and afterwards the ball was auctioned for charity. It was purchased by Mr. Rowland Lishman, who promptly handed it back to be auctioned a second time. The second buyer was Lieutenant Park, who gave the ball to the men of the Duke of Wellington's regiment who were stationed locally.

The day also saw the resolution of the unfinished business between Bolckow, Vaughan and Dorman, Long. The replay took place at South Bank, in aid of the Red Cross and the Soldiers' Parcels Funds, and in an entertaining game Bolckow's won by 2 goals to 1.

On 3rd November 1917 two further first-round ties were decided; Armstrong's Naval Yard and Angus Sanderson's met at Hollymount, the home ground of Bedlington United, in aid of the Scottish Fund, Armstrong's winning emphatically by 4 goals to nil. In the Teesside section Rise Carr defeated Darlington Railway Athletic 3-1, their centre-forward Sarah Hooper scoring all three goals. Hooper was beginning to make a name for herself, having scored 14 goals in four games. She had the pedigree for it; her uncle, Charles Roberts, was an England international who had made 271 appearances for Manchester United before the war, and her brothers, Mark and Bill, would later play for Sheffield Wednesday and Darlington respectively.

Palmer's and Birtley took the field again on 10th November at Chester-le-Street in a bid to settle their undecided round 1 tie. Palmer's took the lead in the first half with goals from M. Dodd and L. Young, with Sally Matthews getting a single goal for Birtley. Just before the end Birtley were awarded a penalty, which Sally Matthews converted. The Palmer's team protested, and walked off the field with three minutes left to play. They had not returned to the pitch when the referee blew for full time, and the incident was reported to the Cup Committee. An emergency meeting took place at Shields Cafe on 13th November, and after considering all the facts the Committee decided to award the tie to Birtley.

The southernmost teams in the region, Skinningrove Ironworks and Ridley's (also based at Skinningrove), had been drawn against each other. The result of their game did not appear in the Teesside or Tyneside newspapers, probably because of their geographical isolation, but from subsequent games we know that Ridley's defeated their neighbours and progressed to the next round.

The postponed tie between Blyth and Aviation Athletic finally took place on 17th November. The venue was New Delaval, and the match was in aid of the local St John's Ambulance Brigade. A large crowd had turned out to see the game, and the receipts were boosted by a cheque for £10 which was handed over by Mr. Tracey, Manager of the Empire Theatre, Blyth.

Although the published draw had pitted Blyth United against the team for Gosforth, it was in fact Blyth Spartans who took the field. It is likely that the published draw was in error, as the Spartans team were far stronger than their neighbours. They quickly proved they were too strong for Aviation too, winning 4-2 in a thrilling game which saw goals from Bella Reay (2), Dolly Allen and Ada Read for Blyth, and E. Waters and E. Reay for Gosforth.

On 24th November Bolckow, Vaughan &. Co. met Ridley's of Skinningrove in a second round tie, and defeated them 4-1 to go into the quarter-finals. The progress of the competition was rapidly becoming disorganised; on the same day, Dorman Long's No. 1 team and Richardson Westgarth's No. 1 team met for the first time in their first round tie. The match took place at the Victoria Ground, Stockton, where a crowd of 2,000 had assembled, and was in aid of the Sailors and Minesweepers' Orphans Fund. The first half was goalless, but early in the second half Dorman's centre-forward, McGuire, made an individual run which she capped with a shot which crept in under the bar. Dorman's continued to press, but Richardsons fought back, and their left winger, O'Neil, equalised with a goal described in the match account as "a beauty".

A second drawn encounter was not reported, and the teams met for a third time on 1st December 1917 at Samuelson's Athletic Ground, Middlesbrough, this time in aid of "Jack's Bairns" and the Soldiers and Sailors Christmas Parcels Funds. A touch of glamour was added by having the game kicked off formally by "Miss Zetta Mor, a star artiste at the Middlesbrough Empire", rather than the usual local dignitary's wife. This diversion had no effect on the result; by now the teams knew each other's game inside out, and a tense 0-0 draw was the outcome, prompting a fourth replay. No record of this match appeared in the newspapers, but one presumes that Dorman's were the eventual winners as they subsequently appeared in the next round.

Over the Christmas and New Year holiday period a number of teams progressed to the third round, but not all the results were reported in the newspapers. Among those which went unreported were: Hood Haggies v Armstrong's Naval Yard (Naval Yard won); Armstrong-Whitworth's 60 Shop v 40 Shop (60 Shop won); Darlington Rise Carr v Richardson, Westgarth No. 2 (Rise Carr won); Stephenson's v Dorman, Long No. 1 (Dorman, Long won). The game between Armstrong-Whitworth's 57 Shop and the Birtley Cartridge Case Factory on 29th December 1917 did make it into the papers - 57 Shop won 1-0.

Another match which was covered by the papers was attended by a fair degree of controversy; On Boxing Day 1917 Dorman Long's No. 2 team met Smith's Dock in the second round at Normanby Road. Heavy snow had fallen, and although the ground staff had made an effort to clear the pitch the markings were largely obscured. The going was heavy, and the Smith's Dock captain had to be carried off after collapsing early on in the game. Because of the conditions the standard of play was poor. The game finished Dorman Long 2 - Smith's Dock 0, whereupon an immediate protest was lodged by the losing side. A meeting of the Cup Committee was convened under the Chairmanship of Mr. T. Pearse of Jarrow, and having considered the complaint, they ordered the match to be replayed. Their decision was made on several grounds; not only were the pitch markings completely obscured by snow and the encroachment of spectators onto the pitch hindered the players, but players and referee alike were pelted by snowballs during the game. Far more serious however was the fact that Dorman's had fielded 12 players for part of the game; one must consider them lucky not to have been disqualified!

It was but a short respite for Smith's Dock; the replay took place at Middlesbrough on 5th January 1918 and once more Dorman's emerged the victors, this time by a margin of 1 goal to nil.

Blyth Spartans were the last team to qualify for the third round, and they did so in style, beating North East Marine 7-1. The game took place on 12th January at St. James's Park, in aid of the Joseph and Jane Cowen Training Home for Disabled Soldiers and Sailors. It was reported that "Spartans were the heavier team," which must have counted in their favour on the heavy, snow-covered pitch. It was a game of high drama; Ada Read opened the scoring for Spartans, and before the interval Bella Reay had added another four goals. Ten minutes after the restart Reay scored again, and a furious protest was mounted by the N.E.M. team, who claimed she had been offside. When the referee refused to change his decision N.E.M. walked off the field. The pitch was invaded by spectators and a heated argument ensued. Meanwhile, behind the scenes the organisers were making frantic efforts to persuade N.E.M. to return, fearing a riot if they refused and the crowd demanded their money back. After an anxious 15 minutes N.E.M. agreed to restart the game, but the farce was not yet over as the referee now refused to take any further part in the proceedings. Fortunately a substitute referee was found and the game continued, Bella Reay rubbing salt in the wound by notching up a seventh goal. Ethel Wilson managed to get one back for N.E.M., but it was too late. Their cup run was over, in circumstances which they could not have imagined, and certainly would have wished to avoid.

The first quarter-final was played on 2nd February 1918 at Scotswood FC's Blaydon Road. It was a "'local derby", the opposing sides being Armstrong-Whitworth's 57 and 60 Shops. 60 Shop took the offensive from the start, and within a few minutes Florrie Taylor had opened their account. 57 Shop had an opportunity to equalise when they were awarded a penalty, but Laura Gould failed to find the net. 60 Shop preserved their lead until half-time, but 57 Shop had been revived by the interval, and staged a number of attacks, one of which led to another penalty award in their favour. This time Ethel Wallace took the spot-kick, and made no mistake. E. Cole then added the winner for 57 Shop, putting them through into the semi-final.

The second quarter-final to be decided was between Darlington Rise Carr and Dorman, Long No. 2. No details of the game were reported other than the result, which was 1-0 in favour of Darlington.

The last two quarter-finals were both decided on 23rd February 1918. In the first, Blyth Spartans and Armstrong's Naval Yard met at the Westoe Ground, South Shields, in aid of the Soldiers' and Sailors' Orphans Fund. Blyth monopolised the play from the start, and their consistent pressure resulted in an early penalty award. Bella Reay stepped up to take the kick, but to the surprise of her team mates and the opposition she failed to score. Not long afterwards she made up for her error with a goal from open play, and a further goal was added by Allen before the interval. Shortly after the restart Reay scored again, and this was the signal for valiant efforts on the part of the Naval Yard to break through the Spartans' defence. The Spartans' back line held firm however, and the game finished 2-1 in their favour.

The second match was between Bolckow,Vaughan and Co. and Dorman, Long No. 1. This was played at Samuelson's Athletic Ground, Middlesbrough. It was a close fought contest, and near to the end of the game the teams were level at one goal apiece, scored by McKenna and Robinson for Bolckow's and Dorman's respectively. With minutes to go a penalty was awarded to Bolckow's, which was converted by their centre-forward, Winnie McKenna. Dorman's lodged an official protest after the game, but the Munitionettes' Cup Committee upheld the referee's decision, and Bolckow's advanced through to the semi-finals.

The semi-finals were played on 9th March 1918. Blyth Spartans faced Armstrong-Whitworth's 60 Shop at St James's Park, while Bolckow, Vaughan & Co. met Rise Carr at Middlesbrough. A crowd of 10,000 made their way to St James's Park to see what promised to be an exciting encounter between two teams with several scalps to their belt. The band from Armstrong-Whitworth's Elswick factory entertained them before the kick-off, which was performed by Miss E.B. Jayne, OBE. From the start the play was fairly even, and both sets of backs were able to cope with probing moves from the opposing forwards. Spartans scored first after 30 minutes through Annie Allen, but 60 Shop stuck to their task, and Ethel Wallace equalised for them before half-time. The ding-dong struggle resumed in the second half, and once again it was the defences of both sides who had the best of the play, with only the occasional thrill to keep the spectators in an enthusiastic mood. With five minutes to go a draw seemed inevitable, but suddenly Bella Reay managed to shake off her markers, and dashing through to the goalmouth scored with a shot that gave the 60 Shop keeper no chance. Armstrong's frantically piled on the pressure in the dying minutes, and forced a corner, but Spartans kept their heads and emerged 2-1 winners at the close.

The match between Bolckow, Vaughan and Rise Carr produced no goals, and must have been an uninspiring encounter, so much so that none of the Teesside papers carried an account of the game, just the score. The teams met again at South Bank a week later, and Darlington were judged the better side in a game "that was fast pace, and some good play was witnessed, but there was a lot of miskicking," according to the South Bank Express. Winnie McKenna scored the only goal in Bolckow's 1-0 win.

The final was fixed for 30th April 1918 at St James's Park. There was high excitement in Blyth at the prospect, and the band of the 3rd Battalion Northumberland Volunteers was given permission by their commanding officer to travel with the team on the 12:30 train from Blyth. Bob Pailor, the pre-war

Newcastle United centre-forward was to referee the game, which would be recorded for posterity by a newsreel company. The team selected to represent Spartans was as follows: Lizzie James, Hannah Malone, Nellie Fairless, Agnes Sample, Martha O'Brien, Bella Metcalfe (capt.), Ada Reed, Annie Allen, Bella Reay, Dollie Allen, Jennie Morgan. The Bolckow, Vaughan team was not published. The game ended in a 0-0 stalemate, which is probably why I have been able to find only one newspaper account of the event. This appeared in the Shields Daily News, and is reproduced below.

BLYTH SPARTANS V BOLCKOW

Weather conditions were no better than Friday when the Bolckow-Vaughan's played the Blyth Spartans for the Tyne, Wear and Tees Munitionettes' Cup Final at St. James's Park, Newcastle, on Saturday. But a crowd of about 15,000 persons assembled, and followed the game with the greatest interest.

A strong opening was made by Blyth, but the Bolckows proved a good match, and when they had once got going proved themselves no easy opponents. No goals were scored in the first half, but there were some exciting moments.

A shot from Reay, the Spartans' centre, bounced on the crossbar, and then Powell, rushing in, all but scored for the Teessiders. A penalty was granted when, during an exciting moment around the Blyth goal, Malone handled.

In the second half Blyth again opened vigorously, but, owing to the smart play of McKenna for the Teessiders, a corner was forced. There followed in quick succession five corners for Bolckow's. Reay would have scored an easy goal for Blyth, but Kirk thwarted her efforts. There was keen play to the last, but no goals were scored.

Needless to say, no trace of the newsreel film can be found. The replay was delayed for some time, due to difficulties encountered in arranging a venue. There seemed to be no difficulties in securing suitable grounds for these matches, so one concludes that the teams themselves were failing to agree. Eventually, on 14th May 1918, the teams finally agreed to replay at Ayresome Park on the following Saturday in aid of the Teesside War Charities. Spartans made one change from the team they had fielded in the first encounter; Mary Lyons of Jarrow was drafted in at inside-left in place of Dolly Allen. The fact that Mary had already played in the tournament for Palmers did not seem to worry the organisers. Another apparent change, at left-back, was the name of Hannah Weir, but this was, in fact, Hannah Malone playing under her newly-married name. The two teams lined up as follows:

Blyth Spartans: Lizzie James, Hannah Weir, Nellie Fairless, Agnes Sample, Martha O'Brien, Bella Metcalfe (capt.), Ada Reed, Annie Allen, Bella Reay, Mary Lyons, Jennie Morgan

Bolckow, Vaughan: Greta Kirk, V. Martin, Amelia Farrell, E. Rowell, Emily Milner, Anne Wharton, Mary Mahon, Mercy Page, Winnie McKenna (capt.), Gladys Reece, A. Leach

22,000 spectators turned up to witness the showdown. Bolckow's won the toss, and Spartans had to kick off facing the sun and the wind. It did not disadvantage them however, and within ten minutes they had taken the lead through Jennie Morgan. Bolckow's made tremendous efforts to equalise, the crowd cheering Winnie McKenna whenever she got the ball, but Martha O'Brien had her well under control and made sure she had no chance to score. The interval came with Spartans still leading by a single goal.

The second half saw Spartans at their very best; their half-back line was solid, not only breaking up the Bolckow attacks but carrying the play forward, which made it possible for their own forwards to maintain a constant level of attacks which the Bolckow defence could not hope to withstand. The Blyth News reported that "Bella Reay and Mary Lyons were in their element, the former completing the hat-trick. The latter was repeatedly cheered to the echo for her work and dribbling, which reached a point of brilliance when, beating four opponents in succession, she dashed through and beat the fifth, the goalkeeper, thus securing the fifth and last goal." After their lacklustre performance in the first meeting this was a tremendous achievement for Spartans.

After the match the Alfred Wood Cup was presented to Bella Metcalfe by Mr. Blake, Chairman of Middlesbrough F.C. who also presented medals to both teams. A more formal presentation took place at the Theatre Royal, Blyth on Friday 31st May 1918, when Jonathan Ridley, President of the Northumberland Football Association, handed the Cup to Mr. R. Thompson, the Secretary of the Blyth Spartans team. In doing so he said that his audience would agree "that if ever there was a team that deserved a set of medals these girls deserved them. They had had many good football teams in Blyth, but never one with the record the ladies possessed. They had won the Ladies' Challenge Cup and had played the whole of their ties away from home. Since August 1917 they had played 30 games, and had won 26, drawn 4 and lost none, and the goal-getter - 'Wor Bella' had scored 133 goals. The team had travelled through the principal parts of the three adjoining counties playing for charity, and the sum reached was over £2,000."

Responding, Mr. Thompson thanked both the Chairman, Colonel Christie, and Mr Ridley for their interest in the team, and also Mr. D. Hardy, who had been so confident in the success of the team that he had offered the use of the theatre for this ceremony long before the close of the competition. They were all very proud of the team's record, which had not been achieved without some sacrifice and self-denial. In closing, he also thanked the public for their support.

From the viewpoint of its charitable objectives the tournament was a huge success. It raised more than £1,500 for various charities, of which the Cup Final at St. James's raised £346 10s 0d, and the replay at Ayresome £325 0s 5d. The latter sum was distributed as follows:- Holgate Red Cross Auxiliary Hospital £60; Riversdale V.A.D. Red Cross Hospital £40; Nurses' Home, Middlesbrough £40; North Ormesby Cottage Hospital £40; North Riding Infirmary £40; South Bank Girl Workers' Rest Club £40; Blyth War Widows' and Orphans' Fund £40; Stockton and Thornaby Hospital £25.

More importantly, the competition had given a great deal of entertainment to the public during a dark period of the war, and a tremendous sense of pride and achievement to the young women who had participated.

The Tyne, Wear and Tees Munitionettes' Cup was confidently claimed to be the first, and only Ladies' Cup competition in existence, but although it may have been the first to be set in motion, another tournament had been the first to get players onto the field. This was the Workington Ladies' Challenge Cup, the first tie of which, between Seaton and Maryport, took place on 15th September 1917. The Cumbrian tournament was smaller, for the reasons mentioned in the previous chapter, and featured only six teams in all. Nevertheless it generated the same degree of passion, which culminated in remarkable scenes after the final at Lonsdale Park, Workington, on 27th October 1917. Under the banner "Uproarious Lady Footballers", the Cumberland News reported that the Mayor, Mr. F. Hall, was shouted down by the players of the losing team, who were from Seaton, as he attempted to present brooches to the winners from Cockermouth. The cause of the disorderly scene was the awarding of a penalty to Cockermouth shortly before half-time, which resulted in the only goal of the game. The Seaton players claimed that the referee had been biassed against them, and in a final display of anger they refused to accept their runners-up brooches. The team itself appears to have disbanded after the affair, as their name does not appear again in the local newspapers.

Chapter 3

Munitionette Internationals

A key figure in the staging of football matches for charity during WW1 was Bill McCracken, the Newcastle United and Ireland full-back. He joined Newcastle in 1904 from Belfast Distillery, and stayed with them until 1923, making 377 appearances in total.

Following the cessation of professional football at the end of the 1914-15 season, McCracken got involved in the organisation of charity matches. The quality of football in these games was higher than one might expect; many former professional footballers were working in the munitions factories, including McCracken himself, and he had the contacts necessary to put together some fairly strong teams, which played under the name of "McCracken's XI". He was involved with munitionettes' games from the very beginning, and acted as referee in the Wallsend Slipway v NEM game on 3rd February 1917, which was the first such game to be reported in the local press. His open-minded attitude to the women's game, coupled with his passion for football and his Northern Ireland connections led him to referee, in December 1917, the first women's international football match between teams of munitionettes from Northern Ireland and the North East of England. It was also a personal watershed for him, as he had only recently been reconciled with the football authorities in Ireland after having refused to turn out for them in an international match before the war.

The date fixed for the encounter was Boxing Day 1917, and a trial match was staged at Wallsend on 15th December 1917 to select a side to represent England. The players were split into two sides - the "Probables" and the "Possibles", comprised as follows:

Probables: May Horn (Slipway), Hilda Weygood (North-Eastern), Maggie Short (Slipway), Mary Mulligan (Slipway), Bella Carrott (North-Eastern), Margaret Hayton (Willington Foundry), Mary Dorrian (West Hartlepool), Nellie Kirk (West Hartlepool), Ethel Jackson (North Eastern), Violet Bryant (Slipway), Lizzie McConnell (Slipway)

Possibles: Maggie Scott (Jarrow), Lepine (Sunderland), Grace Chambers (Slipway), Ettie Catterick (North-Eastern), Bella Reay (Blyth), Bella Turnbull (Slipway), Watson (Hood Haggie), May Grey (Slipway), Sarah Cornforth (Birtley), Connell (Swan and Hunter), Scott (North-Eastern)

The Probables, with the wind at their backs, attacked from the outset, but after Cornforth had twice tested Horn it was the Possibles who opened the scoring through Turnbull. The Probables continued to have the better of play, with Dorrian, Jackson and Kirk getting in a number of shots without being able to find the net. At half-time the Possibles led by 1-0. In the second half the Possibles had a good run of play, but were driven back. Scott had to come out of her goal to clear from Kirk, but shortly afterwards Kirk centred to Bryant who equalised, and the score remained 1-1 till the final whistle. Following the match the organising committee picked the squad to travel to Belfast; it comprised eight probables, four possibles and one member, Bella Willis, who had not taken part in the trial.

The party left Newcastle Central at the unearthly hour of 00:40 on Monday 24th December, accompanied by their Manager, Mr. David Brooks of Rosehill, and Welfare Officer, Nurse Harrison. The journey was eventful; as team captain Bella Carrott later related to her niece, Lily Dunlavery, the Manager got extremely drunk during the sea crossing, and locked himself in the toilet singing "Waiter, waiter, bring me some paper to wipe my bumbelater." (This was probably the same David Brooks who in 1922 promoted the Dick, Kerr Ladies' tour of the United States and Canada, and on the outward journey conned his fellow-passengers into collecting £45 for him by pretending to lose his wallet overboard.)

One hopes that they managed to get some sleep during the journey, because a busy social programme had been organised for them. On the afternoon of the 24th they attended a football match at Grosvenor Park between two local teams, visited a hospital and the cinema, and in the evening were taken to a show at the Belfast Hippodrome. The following day, Christmas Day, they watched Linfield play Distillery in the morning at Grosvenor Park, and were then taken across the city to Windsor Park for the final of the Steel Cup. A dance in the Victoria Hall followed in the evening.

Finally, on Boxing Day morning they got to play some football. At 11:00 the following teams lined up at Grosvenor Park:

England: Maggie Scott, Hilda Weygood, Maggie Short, Bella Willis, Bella Carrott (capt.), Bella Turnbull, Mary Dorrian, Nellie Kirk, Sarah Cornforth, Ethel Jackson, Lizzie McConnell; reserves: Violet Bryant, Ettie Catterick

Ireland: Lennox (Belfast Whites), Osborne (Lurgan Blues), E. Walker (Belfast Whites), Riddell (Belfast Whites), G. Morrow (Belfast Whites, capt.), McCune (Belfast Whites), Cox (Belfast Whites), Montgomery (Belfast Whites), Hall (Lurgan Blues), Burrowes (Belfast Whites), Murphy (Lurgan Blues).

20,000 spectators were in attendance, and as few Tynesiders would have been able to make the trip under wartime conditions the support would have been very one-sided in favour of the Irish team. Bill McCracken had Jimmie Lawrence of Newcastle United, a Scot, and Mick Hamill of Manchester United, an Ulsterman, as linesmen. The Lord Mayor of Belfast kicked off formally, and then the real action started. The Irish team were on the attack from the beginning, and there was great excitement when they narrowly failed to score within minutes of the kick-off. England contained the early attack, and for a while the play was confined to midfield. After ten minutes Mary Dorrian put England ahead, receiving the ball on the right wing and scoring with a high shot into the net. The Irish responded to this challenge, and Montgomery, after slipping a couple of opponents, passed to Hall who levelled the scores with a fine shot. The same player missed an easy opportunity minutes later, and Ireland paid the price, Ethel Jackson restoring the English lead shortly before half-time.

Early in the second half England were awarded a penalty, which was expertly converted by Sarah Cornforth. The play was still very much in England's favour, but the Irish team stuck to their task, and contained them until near the end, when Nellie Kirk added a further goal to make the final result England 4, Ireland 1. Bella Carrott, the English captain, was judged the best player on the field by the Daily Chronicle.

Lizzie McConnell, speaking many years later, recalled that on the return journey the team were in a state of nervous anxiety due to the sighting of what was thought to be a German submarine. Whether this caused the manager to resort to the bottle again is not known.

Two further international matches were to take place; on 20th July 1918 the North of England met the West of Scotland at St. James's Park, Newcastle, in aid of the St. Dunstan's home for Blinded Soldiers and Sailors. There were a number of changes in the English side, which comprised the following:

Jennie Hodge (Middlesbrough), Hilda Weygood (Wallsend N.E.M.), Nellie Fairless (Blyth Spartans), Bella Willis (60 Shop A.W. & Co. and Prudhoe), Sarah Cornforth (Birtley and Pelton), Minnie Seed (Armstrong's Naval Yard, late Gosforth Aviation and Sunderland), Mary Dorrian (Brown's, West Hartlepool), Winnie McKenna (Bolckow's, South Bank, capt.), Bella Reay (Blyth Spartans), Mary Lyons (Palmer's Jarrow), Lizzie McConnell (Wallsend Slipway)

Scotland's team was also made up of Munitions workers, the line-up being as follows:

Jean Brown (Cardonald, Govan), Dolly Cookson (Inchinnan, Paisley, late capt. Vickers FC Barrow), Rosina Clark (Clydesdale), Jean Wilson (Cardonald, Glasgow), Agnes Connell (Mossend, Carfin), Bella Renwick (Mossend, Motherwell), Robina Murdock (Mossend, Motherwell), Nellie McKenzie (Cardonald, Glasgow), Lizzie McWilliams (Clydesdale).

The game was kicked off, as usual, by a celebrity, this time in the person of Miss Hetty King, who was appearing at the Empire Theatre. One wonders if this was an attempt at whimsical humour on the part of the organisers, as Hetty King (real name Winifred Emms), was a famous male impersonator, whose best-known song was "All the nice girls love a sailor."

There was nothing false about the action which followed, however. Women's football had moved on from the days when crowds came to laugh at their efforts, and the game was described as "one of the best of its kind seen at Newcastle... the football was fairly fast and some really clever work was witnessed." The Scottish players in particular approached the game in a robust fashion, and one of their number had to be spoken to by the referee.

Scotland took the lead with a soft goal from Agnes Connell, but Winnie McKenna, the hotshot from South Bank, equalised with a goal that was described as a beauty. England got two more before the interval, Sarah Cornforth consolidating her reputation as a penalty ace, and then a free-kick let in Mary Lyons of Jarrow, who scored just before the interval. In doing so she established another sadly unrecognised record - she was only 14 years old, and remains to this day the youngest player not only to play for, but to score for England in a senior international.

In the second half both sides were awarded penalties. Bella Willis, rather than Sarah Cornforth, took England's kick, and missed, but Maggie Devlin was on the mark for the Scots, reducing England's lead to a single goal. The Scots piled on the pressure, and England nearly threw the game away in the last few minutes, but there was no further score and the final result remained North of England 3, West of Scotland 2. The best players were judged to be Lyons, Dorrian, McKenna and Cornforth for England, and Brown, Cookson, Murdoch and Devlin for Scotland.

The final international game played by North East Munitionettes was a return match against Ireland on 21st September 1918. This time St James's Park was the venue, the charitable cause being the Lord Mayor's War Relief Fund. The organisers decided to include the football match as part of an International Sports Gala, with an 80 yards sprint, a tug-of-war and a penalty kick competition preceding the main event. Only 2,000 spectators turned up, compared to the 20,000 who had witnessed the first meeting of these sides, but this may have been due to the serious influenza epidemic which was sweeping the country at the time.

Several of the players took part in the penalty kick competition, which was won, somewhat predictably, by Sarah Cornforth. One of the goalkeepers was Newcastle United's Jimmy Lawrence, who was to referee the main event, and many years later Sarah Cornforth would still boast of having beaten the United keeper with a penalty at St James's.

Before the game the following teams were published:

England: Scott (Jarrow), Weygood (Wallsend), Jackson (Wallsend), Willis (Prudhoe, capt.), Cornforth (West Pelton), Carrot (Gateshead), Dorrian (Hartlepool), Kirk (Hartlepool), McKenna (South Bank), Seed (Sunderland), McConnell (Rose Hill).

Ireland: Fisher (Belfast), Walker (Belfast), Moffat (Belfast), Ridell (Belfast, capt.), Forsyth (Ewart's, Antrim), McEwan (Belfast), Martin (Enniskillen), McLatchie (Portadown), Hall (Lurgan), Knox (Ewarts), Dolan (Belfast).

Two members of the England side failed to turn up, and Mary Lyons of Palmer's was drafted in as one of the substitutes.

The game was kicked off by the Irish team manager, Mrs Walter Scott, in the absence of the Lord Mayor. From the commencement of the game England played with greater skill, Lyons and McKenna in particular giving the Irish defence a hard time. Lyons scored England's first when the Irish goalkeeper failed to come forward and clear the ball, and then McKenna added a second, racing in between the backs to slot home a long drive. The Irish play picked up for a while, but Willis and Cornforth were rock steady in England's defence. Eventually Ruby Hall managed to score for the visitors, but almost immediately Nellie Kirk added a third for England.

England dominated in the second half, and Fisher and her two full backs were kept busy, but could not prevent Lyons and McKenna each scoring again. Shortly before the final whistle Hall got a second for Ireland, to make the final score England 5, Ireland 2.

Because of the poor attendance the takings at the gate amounted to only £60. The organisers were faced with making a loss, but Newcastle United came to the rescue, and agreed to waive their fee for the use of the ground.

Opinions may differ on whether these games qualify as the first-ever women's football internationals. The Football Association accords this honour to a game played between the Dick, Kerr & Co. Ladies of Preston, and a touring French team, which took place at Deepdale in April 1920. One would not wish to diminish the achievements of the Dick, Kerr team, to whom women's football today owes such a legacy. Nevertheless, the games played by the north east

Munitionettes have a greater claim to be regarded as true internationals, as in each case both teams were representative of their regions, whereas the Dick, Kerr team was purely a club side.

Similarly, a match played at Celtic Park, Glasgow, on 2nd March 1918 which was billed as "Scotland v England" was actually between the works teams of Vickers-Maxim at Barrow-in-Furness and Beardmore's at Parkhead. The Vickers team won 4-0 with goals from Dickinson (2), Bradley and an own goal.

Chapter 4

County and District Matches

In the early years of the twentieth century inter-County football was still highly regarded, even within the professional game. The formation of the Munitionettes' Cup Committee provided the impetus, and the facility, to organise women's matches at this level. These would bring together the top players from all the works teams, ensuring a higher standard of football, and attracting larger crowds, to the benefit of the charitable causes they supported. The other great rivalries which could also be exploited were those existing between the three main centres of population - Teesside, Tyneside and Wearside.

The first inter-district match to be reported took place on 22nd December 1917 when teams representing Teesside and Wearside met at the Sunderland Rovers ground in Hendon. The teams lined up as follows:

Teesside: A. Briggs (Dorman's, Clarence), B. Quigley (Richardson Westgarth's No. 1), A. Dukes (Dorman's No. 1), Amelia Farrell (Bolckow's), R. Boyle (Dorman's Port Clarence), L. Robson (Dorman's Port Clarence), Sarah English (Smith's Dock), Gertie Jefferson (Richardson Westgarth's No. 1), Winnie McKenna (capt., Bolckow's), Mabel McKinstry (Dorman's No. 2) and A. Leach (Bolckow's)

Wearside: Scott or Adamson (Glaholm & Robson), N. English (Sunderland Ladies), Alice Kidney (Webster's), S. McCormack (Sunderland Ladies), G. Hooton (Glaholm & Robson), B. Halliday (Webster's), M. McCulley (Webster's), Amy Smith (Sunderland Ladies), V. Lowson (Webster's), G. Lincoln and S. Patterson (Glaholm & Robson).

The Teesside team were evidently the more experienced, their play being more organised and their kicking of the ball noticeably stronger. In the first half play was confined almost entirely to the Wearside half of the field, the home team only occasionally managing to get near the Teesside goal by rushing. Teesside were the first to score through Leach, McKenna adding a second, which was followed almost immediately by a third from Jefferson. During one of their periodic rushes upfield Wearside managed to pull one back with a fine goal from Lawson. The end of the first half was livened up by a fight which broke out between two of the girls, the referee having to step in to calm things down. In the second half play was more even. McKenna got one more goal for the visitors, and substitute Whiteside, who had replaced English, scored another for Wearside, making the final score Wearside 2 - Teesside 4.

Four days later, as mentioned in the previous chapter, the Tyneside team successfully took on a Northern Ireland eleven in Belfast. It was inevitable therefore that an early meeting would be arranged between Tyneside and Teesside, to settle the question of which of them could be regarded as North East champions. The teams selected to represent their respective areas were as follows, Tyneside making seven changes from that which had faced Northern Ireland:

Tyneside: Maggie Scott (Palmers Jarrow), Julia Turnbull (Birtley), Florrie Deardon (Hood Haggies), Bella Willis (60 Shop), Bella Carrot capt. (NEM), Martha Lothian (57 Shop), Bella Thompson (Naval Yard), Ethel Jackson (NEM), Bella Reay (Blyth Spartans), Minnie Seed (Gosforth Aviation) and Agnes McConnell (Wallsend Slipway)

Teesside: V. Hodge (Dorman's No. 1), Amelia Farrell (Bolckow's), Emily Ashton (Darlington), A. Appleton (Darlington), M. O'Connell (Westgarth's No. 2), Anne Wharton (Darlington), L. Dunne (Dorman's No. 2), Gertie Jefferson (Westgarth's No. 1, capt.), Winnie McKenna (Bolckow's), Mabel McKinstry (Dorman's No. 2), A. Leach (Bolckow's)

The day for the encounter was originally set for 19th January 1918, but adverse weather conditions resulted in a postponement. It eventually kicked off on 2nd February 1918 at the Victoria Ground, Stockton, before a crowd of 2,000, the proceeds going to the Soldiers' and Sailors' Parcels Fund. Bob Pailor, the Stockton-born Newcastle United centre-forward acted as referee. To improve the spectators' enjoyment of the game, the players wore numbers on the back of their jerseys, and a match programme (included in the entry price of 6d) was printed to allow individual players to be identified from their number. This was yet another first for munitionettes' football - players' numbers were not used in the Football League until 1928, and did not become mandatory until 1939.

For the first 15 minutes Tyneside had all the play, poor passing on the part of the Teesside players preventing them from making the most of the opportunities which fell their way. About five minutes from the interval Bella Reay scored with a fine shot to open the account for Tyneside. Teesside made a much better showing in the second half, but the Tyneside defence was never found wanting. However, a tremendous solo effort by McKenna saw her cover half the length of the field, and she rounded off her run with a neatly-placed left-foot shot which gave Scott no chance. The celebrations which followed this goal would have done justice to the modern day professional game. In the closing minutes Tyneside nearly scored again, but the match finished at one goal apiece. For the time being, the question as to which was the top team in the North East remained unanswered.

The replay took place at St. James's Park on Saturday March 2nd, in aid of St. Dunstan's Hostel for Blinded Soldiers and Sailors. Both teams had made a number of changes to their line-ups, but the two goalscorers from the first encounter both held their places.

Tyneside (green and white): Lizzie James (Blyth Spartans), Florrie Deardon (Hood, Haggie's), Maggie Short (Wallsend Slipway), Lizzie Form (Palmer's), Sarah Cornforth (Birtley), Martha Lothian (57 Shop), Ada Reed (Blyth Spartans), Ethel Jackson (NEM), Bella Reay (Blyth Spartans), Minnie Seed (Gosforth Aviation), Hilda Ruddock (Armstrong's Naval Yard)

Teesside (scarlet and white): Jennie Hodge (Dorman, Long & Co.), Amelia Farrell (Bolckow, Vaughan & Co.), A Dukes (Dorman, Long & Co.), M. O'Connell (Richardson, Westgarth's & Co.), R. Boyle (Dorman, Long & Co.), Jessie Lodge (Darlington), N. Humphries (Dorman, Long & Co.), Gertie Jefferson (Richardson, Westgarth's & Co.), Winnie McKenna (Bolckow, Vaughan & Co.), Mabel McKinstry (Dorman, Long & Co.), A. Leach (Bolckow, Vaughan & Co.)

Surprisingly, the local newspapers did not carry a report of the game, the only record being of the final score, which was 3-0 in favour of Tyneside.

Having settled, temporarily, the Tyneside v Teesside issue, it was time for the Durham v Northumberland rivalry to be contested. The first inter-county munitionettes game took place at St. James's Park on Good Friday, 29th March 1918, in aid of the Joseph and Jane Cowen Home for the Retraining of Disabled Servicemen. The teams which took the field contained many familiar names from the Tyneside-Teesside encounters, but now with different loyalties. The selection of a player was based upon the county of their birth, not the location of their works team.

Durham: Maggie Scott (Foster, Blackett & Wilson), Bella Smith (Angus Sanderson), Julia Turnbull (Birtley CC), Lizzie Form (Palmer's Jarrow), Bella Carrott (North Eastern Marine), J. Miller (58 Shop Scotswood), Mary Dorrian (Brown's, West Hartlepool), Nellie Kirk (Brown's, West Hartlepool), Sarah Cornforth (Birtley CC), Minnie Seed (Gosforth Aviation), Hilda Ruddock (Walker Naval Yard)

Northumberland: N. Heron (Walker Naval Yard), Florrie Deardon (Hood, Haggie's, Willington), Maggie Short (Wallsend Slipway), Bella Willis (60 Shop), Ettie Andrews (57 Shop), B. Wallace (Wallsend Slipway), Ella Fairbairn (57 Shop), Ethel Wallace (57 Shop), Sarah Henderson (58 Shop), Ethel Jackson (North East Marine), Lizzie McConnell (Wallsend Slipway)

Despite inclement weather on the day of the match, some 5,000 spectators made their way to St. James's Park to see what the Northern Echo described as "a hard encounter." Northumberland took the initiative from the start, their wingers in particular making numerous openings, despite some fierce challenges from the Durham backs. The first goal was scored by Ethel Wallace to put Northumberland ahead. Durham responded with a wave of attacks, marshalled by captain Cornforth, who found the net three times before the interval to put Durham two goals to the better. The beginning of the second half was characterised by some very fast play, with Durham having the better of the exchanges. The Northumberland half-backs were solid in defence, but were less effective in feeding the ball to their forwards. Sarah Cornforth was judged the best player on the day, and she scored once more for her team, this time from a penalty. In the last half-hour Northumberland had a number of chances, and twice Ethel Jackson was clean through with only the goalkeeper to beat, but she shot wide on both occasions, and the final score remained 4-1 in favour of Durham.

The munitionette teams on Wearside lacked the strength in depth of their counterparts on the Tyne and Tees, and for their return match against Teesside on 20th April 1918 they selected 6 guest players from Tyneside teams, the justification being that these players originated from the Wearside area:

Wearside: M. Jane (Armstrong's Naval Yard), N. English (Sunderland), Alice Kidney (Webster's), Lizzie Form (Palmer's), E. Lister (Naval Yard), B. Halliday (Webster's), H. Noble (Sunderland), Ethel Wallace (Armstrong-Whitworth), V. Lowson (Webster's), Minnie Seed (Gosforth Aviation), Hilda Ruddock (Naval Yard);

Teesside: J. Hawthorn (Richardson Westgarth No. 1), Amelia Farrell (Bolckow, Vaughan), Emily Ashton (Darlington), A. Hartley (Smith's Dock), Jennie Lodge (Darlington), Anne Wharton (Bolckow, Vaughan), Lillian Dunne, Mabel McKinstry (both Dorman, Long No. 2), Winnie McKenna (Bolckow, Vaughan), Gertie Jefferson (Richardson Westgarth No. 1), A. Dukes (Dorman, Long No. 1)

Several thousand spectators braved hail, snow and rain to make their way to the Normanby Road ground, South Bank, but the weather had deteriorated so badly by the kick-off that the game was abandoned before it started. It was rescheduled at the same venue a fortnight later, on 4th May 1918. Wearside won the toss, and kicked off, but Teesside soon took the attack. The forwards of both teams played well but the backs were observed to be "rather off colour," according to the South Bank Express. Teesside scored twice in the first halfthrough Jefferson and Dunne, and then Winnie McKenna got a brace in the second half, to emphasise Teesside's superiority once more with a 4-0 win.

A regional game with a difference took place on 1st June 1918. On this occasion the opposing sides were billed as the Tyneside Internationals versus the North of England. The good folk of Hartlepool might have felt a little aggrieved at this, as two of the "Tyneside Internationals" came from their town. The match was played at St. James's Park in aid of the Comrades of the Great War, and more than £100 was taken at the turnstiles, suggesting a crowd of between 5,000 and 6,000. The teams were as follows:

Tyneside: Maggie Scott (Foster Blacketts), Hilda Weygood (N.E.M.), Maggie Short (Wallsend Slipway), Bella Willis (60 Shop, Scotswood), Bella Carrott capt. (N.E.M.), Violet Bryant (Wallsend Slipway), Mary Dorrian, Nellie Kirk (both Brown's, West Hartlepool), Sarah Cornforth (Birtley), Ethel Jackson (N.E.M.), Lizzie McConnell (Wallsend Slipway)

North of England: Ada Shaw (60 Shop & Rowlands Gill), Laura Gould (57 Shop & Scotswood), Amelia Farrell (Bolckows, South Bank), Nellie Stott (Browns, West Hartlepool), Bella Plummer (Expansion, West Hartlepool), Jessie Lodge (Darlington), Lilian Dunne (Middlesbrough), Ethel Wallace (57 Shop & Newcastle), Winnie McKenna (Bolckows, South Bank), Minnie Seed (Sunderland & Aviation), Hilda Ruddock (Naval Yard & Ryhope)

The teams were well-matched, and more than 25 minutes passed before a goal was scored. Nellie Kirk, playing for the Internationals, sent in a shot which Ada Shaw scrambled to clear, but in doing so put through her own goal. Goalkeeper error was also to blame for the equaliser, scored five minutes into the second half, when Maggie Scott carried the ball outside her area. A free kick was awarded against her for handball, from which Winnie McKenna scored. Later the Internationals were awarded a penalty, which Sarah Cornforth converted, but they were denied victory when Winnie McKenna got her second, making the final result 2-2.

The contest for supremacy between Tyneside and Teesside resumed on 15th June 1918. Again the venue was St. James's Park, and this time the match was in aid of the Northumberland Prisoners of War Fund. The Munitionettes' Cup Committee extended a special invitation to wounded soldiers and sailors, who would, it was announced, be admitted to the grandstand free. The game was a dull affair however, and a goalless draw was the outcome.

Following the match on 1st June the representatives from Hartlepool must have aired their views on the so-called "Tyneside Internationals", for when a rematch took place on 6th July 1918 the team was simply labelled the "Internationals".

Internationals: Maggie Scott (Foster Blacketts), Hilda Weygood (N.E.M.), Ethel Jackson (Wallsend Slipway), Bella Willis (60 Shop, Scotswood), Bella Carrott capt. (N.E.M.), Bella Turnbull (Wallsend Slipway), Mary Dorrian, Nellie Kirk (both West Hartlepool), Sarah Cornforth (Birtley), Violet Bryant (Wallsend Slipway), Lizzie McConnell (Wallsend Slipway)

North of England: Ada Shaw (60 Shop and Rowlands Gill), Grace Battista (60 Shop, Scotswood), Emily Ashton (Darlington), Nellie Stott (West Hartlepool), Jessie Lodge (Darlington), Annie Wharton (South Bank), Minnie Seed (Armstrong's Naval Yard and Sunderland), Winnie McKenna (South Bank), Bella Reay (Blyth Spartans), Mary Lyons (Palmer's, Jarrow), Ethel Wallace (57 Shop, Scotswood)

St James's Park was the venue once more, the proceeds being for the benefit of the Y.W.C.A. and Munitionettes' Funds. A crowd of 4,000 watched the game, and were amazed at the ball skills of the 14-year-old prodigy from Jarrow, Mary Lyons. The Daily Chronicle considered her the best player on the pitch, but noted that she had no luck with her shooting. Once again the teams proved to be well matched, with goals from Nellie Stott for the North of England, and Alice Churcher, a late substitute for the Internationals, contributing to a 1-1 draw.

Durham and Northumberland confronted each other once more on 7th September 1918, this time at the Rockcliffe ground, Monkseaton, in aid of the Monkseaton branch of Comrades of the Great War, the result on this occasion being an emphatic 3-0 win for Durham. Durham's ascendancy seemed to be well established by this result, but they experienced a reversal a month later when Northumberland defeated them 1-0 at St. James's Park on 12th October 1918. The Northumberland team included five members from Blyth Spartans, which no doubt contributed to their success on this occasion.

Durham: Ada Wildman (Annfield Plain), Bella Smith (Close Works, Gateshead), Lizzie Gibson (Palmer's Jarrow), Lily Proud (Haggie Bros, Gateshead), Bella Carrot (NEM and Gateshead), Lizzie Sawyers (F. B. & W. Hebburn), Mary Dorrian (West Hartlepool), Nellie Kirk (West Hartlepool), Lizzie E Lowes (Angus Sanderson and Wrekenton), Mary Lyons (Palmer's, Hebburn), Minnie Seed (Palmer's and Sunderland).

Northumberland: Sarah Atkinson (N.U.T. Benwell), Grace Battista (A. W. & Co. 60 Shop, Newcastle), Nellie Fairless (Blyth Spartans), Bella Willis (Prudhoe, capt.), Martha O'Brien (Blyth Spartans), Cissie Short (A. W. & Co. 58 Shop), Flo Wallace (Wallsend), Annie Allen (Blyth Spartans), Bella Reay (Blyth Spartans), Ethel Wallace (A. W. & Co. 57 Shop), Jennie Morgan (Blyth Spartans)

A match took place on 14th December 1918 which appeared, on the face of it, to fall into this category. The Newcastle newspapers reported that Tyneside defeated Hartlepool 4-0 at St James's Park, with goals from Bella Reay (2) and Mary Lyons (2), but according to the Northern Daily Mail the so-called Hartlepool team was actually Brown's Sawmills Munition Girls.

Boxing Day 1918 witnessed a clash between the Munitionettes of Tyneside and Whitehaven. The Whitehaven team had a undefeated record; of 25 matches played they had won 23 and drawn two, and one of the notable scalps they had captured was that of the Dick, Kerr Ladies of Preston, whom they had defeated 2-0 at Deepdale on 9th October 1918. The reputation of the visitors drew a crowd of 18,000 to St. James's Park, and the local fans were not disappointed as Tyneside defeated Whitehaven 3-0 with goals from Mary Dorrian, Winnie McKenna and Mary Lyons.

Tyneside: Sarah Atkinson (N.U.T., South Benwell), Grace Battista (A. W. & Co.), Lizzie Gibson (Palmers), Bella Willis (A. W. & Co. and Prudhoe), Cissie Short (A. W. & Co.), Lizzie Form (Palmers), Mary Dorrian (Brown's West Hartlepool), Winnie McKenna (South Bank), Bella Reay (Blyth Spartans), Mary Lyons (Palmers), Minnie Seed (Sunderland).

Whitehaven: Kitty Cowie, May Elwood, Cissie Spedding, Ida Robinason, Winnie Whirity (capt.), Gladys Field, Elsie Lowes, Maggie Cunningham, Vera Wilson, Mary Milne.

A rematch took place at Whitehaven on 18th January 1919, and this time the result was a 1-1 draw, Tyneside's goal coming from Bella Reay.

By now the effects of "demobilisation" had taken their toll, and many of the works teams had ceased to exist. The Munitionettes' Committee were still able, however, to put together representative sides from the region, and on 8th March 1919 a team billed as "Newcastle Ladies" stepped on to the turf at Deepdale to take on the mighty Dick, Kerr side. Once again the description of the team was inaccurate, as four of the players came from Jarrow, two from Hartlepool and one from South Bank. The Preston team were taking no chances, and strengthened their squad with three players from Bolton Ladies, including their captain, Rawsthorne.

Dick, Kerr: Annie Hastie, Alice Kell (capt.), Hulme, Rawsthorne, Jessie Warmsley, Lily Jones, Walker, Jennie Harris, Nellie Mitchell, Minnie Partington, Florrie Redford; reserves: Crawshaw, A. Standing, Elsie Arnold and Dickinson.

Newcastle: Sarah Atkinson, Catherine Egan, Lizzie Gibson, Bella Willis, Cissie Short, Lizzie Form, Mary Dorrian, Nellie Kirk, Winnie McKenna, Mary Lyons, Minnie Seed.

The game was played before a crowd of 5,000, raising £179 for charity, but the conditions were poor and the ground was heavy. The Newcastle team had had a tiring journey overnight, and playing in unfamiliar claret and white stripes they failed to live up to expectations. Mitchell scored the only goal of the game for Dick, Kerr, and the visitors lost their unbeaten record.

Local pride needed to be salved, and it was with keen anticipation that a crowd estimated at between 25,000 and 30,000 packed into St. James's Park for the rematch on 24th April 1919. The North East team had four changes from the one defeated at Preston with the inclusion of Florrie Holmes (Brown's), Grace Battista (Armstrong-Whitworth), Martha O'Brien and Bella Reay (Blyth Spartans) in place of Atkinson, Gibson, Short and Kirk.

Newcastle: Florrie Holmes, Grace Battista, Catherine Egan, Bella Willis (capt.), Martha O'Brien, Lizzie Form, Mary Dorrian, Winnie McKenna, Bella Reay, Mary Lyons, Minnie Seed.

Dick, Kerr: Annie Hastie, Hulme, Alice Kell (capt.), Lily Jones, Jessie Walmsley, Rawsthorne, Florrie Redford, Minnie Partington, Jennie Harris, A. Standing, Molly Walker.

As with so many eagerly-anticipated events, the contest was poor entertainment, being described as "dull and scrambling in comparison with some of the games amongst the fair sex in the past season or two." With honour at stake neither side was taking chances, and the quality of the football was rated as poorer than that exhibited in the Munitionettes' Cup Final earlier in the season. The North Mail picked out the Dick, Kerr left winger, Minnie Partington, for special mention, noting that she had only one superior on the field - Mary Lyons, who, "gave constant evidence of coaching in certain little tricks that would not have disgraced a male player." On one occasion she sent in a fierce shot which the Dick, Kerr goalkeeper just managed to turn over the bar. Despite numerous chances the Newcastle side found it impossible to get the ball into the back of the net, both McKenna and Reay missing good scoring opportunities. The final result, a draw, was probably a fair reflection of the relative merits of the two sides, but the spectacle would have been greatly improved if the score had been other than 0-0.

Three other matches ought to be mentioned here, which strictly speaking were neither inter-County or inter-Regional affairs, but which took on that dimension due to the status of the teams involved. The sides in question represented the two great northern armaments manufacturers - Armstrong-Whitworth of Tyneside and Vickers-Maxim of Barrow-in-Furness. Their first encounter, at St. James's Park on 1st December 1917, attracted 14,000 spectators, and resulted in a 2-1 win for Armstrong-Whitworth, with goals from Sarah Cornforth (penalty) and Bella Willis. The Barrow Times petulantly remarked that Armstrong's had chosen their team from 17 factories, which was stretching things a little; the company had five main centres of operation, albeit with an enormous pool of labour, but at the end of the day the team was still restricted to eleven players. Although the result went against them, there can be no doubt that the Vickers' team enjoyed their visit; the night before the match they were housed in the Douglas Hotel, Grainger Street, and after post-match refreshments at Armstrong's sports club their train pulled out of Newcastle Central Station to the strains of "Will ye no' come back again" from their hosts. They were to come back again, but not immediately, as fair play required that the next encounter take place at Barrow. The game was played at Holker Street, the home of Barrow F.C., on 12th January 1918. Unfortunately heavy snow fell in the morning, and increased in severity prior to the match, which both reduced the prospective attendance and made playing conditions difficult. The teams were as follows:

Vickers: J. Percival, G. Tindall, L. Wagstaff, M. Christian, L. Michaelson, S. McLellan, A. Fletcher, W. Bradley, M. Holmes, L. Parton, M. Dickinson

Armstrong-Whitworth: Ada Shaw (60 Shop), Grace Battista (60 Shop), Julia Turnbull (Birtley CCF), R. Cole (60 Shop), Bella Willis (60 Shop), N. Innes (57 Shop), Lizzie Spedding (Gosforth Aviation), Ella Fairbairn (57 Shop), Sarah Cornforth (Birtley CCF), Ethel Wallace (57 Shop), Hilda Ruddock (Walker Naval Yard)

The snow continued to fall after the start of the game, but the players battled on despite the conditions. Both goals came under pressure on several occasions, but the respective defences dealt with the threat. As the snow ceased, more spectators began to arrive and cheer on the home team, and after 25 minutes play Parton scored for Vickers after a goalmouth scramble.

Conditions had improved somewhat by the commencement of the second half, and the crowd was treated to some entertaining play, the highlight of which was a solo run by Bradley who took the ball over half the length of the field before crashing in Vicker's second goal. Both Cornforth and Ruddock made some outstanding efforts on the part of Armstrong's, but could not get the ball past Percival, and as the final whistle blew Vickers were still leading 2-0.

The usual post-match refreshments and speeches took place after the game, and each member of the visiting team was presented with a pearl and ruby pendant set in gold, provided by W.T. Storey, a local jeweller. Miss E. B. Jayne, speaking on behalf of the visiting team, thanked the people of Barrow for their hospitality and a sporting contest. They accepted that the better team had won on the day, but reminded them that "we licked you in Newcastle," and there would now have to be a third game to decide who was to be "top dog."

Some considerable time was to elapse before the teams could meet again to decide the issue, but eventually a decider was arranged at St. James's Park on 23rd November 1918. The proceeds were to be devoted to a fund to help female munition workers "whose health is suffering by the strain of their work to take necessary rest and recuperation." The players and spectators alike were more interested in who would win.

Armstrong-Whitworth: Ada Shaw (60 Shop), Grace Battista (60 Shop), Julia Turnbull (Birtley CCF), R. Cole (60 Shop), Bella Willis (60 Shop), N. Innes (58 Shop), Lizzie Spedding (Gosforth Aviation), Ella Fairbairn (57 Shop), Sarah Cornforth (Birtley CCF), Ethel Wallace (57 Shop), Hilda Ruddock (Walker Naval Yard)

Vickers: J. Percival, L. Wagstaff, L. Michaelson, A. Fletcher, M. Holmes, D. Cookson, M Christian, S. McLellan, W. Bradley, L. Parton, M. Dickinson

The above teams were posted in the Daily Chronicle on the day of the match, but the account of the game in the Barrow News reveals that Vickers had four players, Wilson, Harris, Bayley and Milmine, whose names do not appear in this line-up. Bayley and Milmine were playing in public for the first time, which must have been a nerve-racking experience, even though the crowd only numbered 5,000.

Vickers showed strongly from the kick-off and early in the game Bayley gave the Armstrong team a nervous moment by striking the foot of the upright. There was no scoring until five minutes before the interval, when Willis sent in a long range shot which Wilson cleared, but before she could get back into her goalmouth Cornforth got the ball into the net for Armstrongs. Towards the close Vicker's came within an ace of equalising, when Christian passed to Harris, who was well placed in front of goal, but before she could shoot Parton rushed in and skied the ball over the bar.

During the customary post-match speeches it was suggested that there ought to be a fourth and final encounter on a neutral ground, but whether this actually took place or not is unknown. Given the speedy discharge of munitionettes from employment following the end of the war it is highly improbable.

Chapter 5

The Munitionettes' Cup 1918-19

When the Munitionettes' Cup Committee met in October 1918 to organise the tournament for a second season, it was already clear that the Allies had won the war. The German Army under Ludendorff had made a final major counter-attack in the 3rd Battle of the Aisne (May 27th - June 6th) but his forces had been halted at the Marne. The summer had witnessed United States troops arriving in Europe at the rate of 10,000 per day, and it became evident to the Central Powers that the game was up. Bulgaria surrendered to the Allies on September 30th, and both Austria and Turkey were crumbling in the face of determined Allied offensives. Germany itself was exhausted, and the only question outstanding was the terms on which an Armistice would be signed. Already the Allied requirement for munitions was diminishing, and it was uncertain whether the munitionettes themselves would continue to be employed for much longer.

The organisation of the tournament was thrown into a state of disarray by the signing of an Armistice on 11th November 1918. The Great War, which had cost millions of lives, overthrown dynasties, and swept away many established social conventions, was finally over. As the guns fell silent the factories which had fed them faced the loss of major supply contracts, and the laying-off of workers was inevitable. Women's jobs were particularly at risk; prior to the war these had mostly been filled by men, and it was taken for granted that when the fighting men returned from the field they would be given priority in employment.

The Government hoped to effect this transition in an orderly manner, and on the very day that the Armistice was signed a directive went out from the Ministry of Munitions to all contractors and sub-contractors; there was to be no general discharge of munitions workers, but those who wished to move jobs were now free to do so, without the necessity of obtaining a permit. Production was to be scaled down by the immediate cessation of overtime and the transfer of workers from piece rates to time rates.

A scheme of non-contributory unemployment benefit was also to be introduced for workers above the age of 18. Men would receive 24s per week, and women 20s for a period of 13 weeks (discharged soldiers could claim up to 26 weeks). Child benefit of 6s per week for the first child and 3s for each subsequent child would also be paid.

How diligently employers adhered to the letter and spirit of this directive is unclear. When the scheme commenced on 25th November 1918 the Daily

Chronicle reported that large numbers of women had registered at the Labour Exchange in Newcastle, but very few men. It commented, "It is thought that in this district there will be little difficulty in finding employment for the men, but a great problem is presented in the case of the women workers." Some employers approached the problem with a positive and enlightened attitude. Foster, Blackett and Wilson converted part of their factory into a toy-manufacturing company which traded under the name Bairntoys, specifically to provide jobs for their female munition workers. However, it is beyond doubt that there was a great lay-off of female workers.

The National Federation of Women Workers urged Newcastle Council to put pressure on the Government to find jobs for unemployed women. The reaction in some quarters was not entirely sympathetic; Councillor W. Ellis complained that his wife had been trying for three weeks to hire a maid and had failed, despite contacting all the registry offices. His sentiments were echoed by D. Humphry of the Gateshead Labour Party, who stated that "the majority of women would prefer domestic service to factory if the conditions were reasonably improved." This was a common attitude within male society, and one which demonstrated a complete lack of understanding of the female viewpoint - women detested domestic service, particularly the "live-in" variety, not only because of the poor wages (as little as 5s per week plus board), but also for the servility and lack of independence it imposed upon them. It would take several more years and another World War before the message finally started to get through.

The Munitionettes' Cup Committee had pressed ahead with organising the competition, but it was clear from the outset that it would not be on the scale of the first. On 7th October 1918, with only 1 week to go before the official close, only 15 companies had submitted entries, which, since some had more than one side, probably represented around 18 teams in total. The Northern Echo reported the following list of interested parties: Blyth Spartans, Darlington Rise Carr, Armstrong-Whitworth 43, 57 and 58 Shops, Lyddite Filling Factory (Lemington), N.U.T. Motor Works (South Benwell), Wallsend Slipway, North East Marine, Foster, Blackett & Wilson, Horden K.C.O. Girls, Brown's (West Hartlepool), Ashmore, Benson Pease & Co. (Stockton), Richardson, Westgarth (Hartlepool) and Dorman, Long & Co. The draw was fixed for Monday 16th October, but no report of it appeared in the newspapers. Whether it went ahead at this time is unknown; the events unfolding in Europe were obviously of greater importance and very few column inches were devoted to sporting matters. One can make only a partial reconstruction of the progress of the competition through those games which were reported.

Round 1 ties:

On 2nd November 1918 Haggie Brothers (Gateshead) and Armstrong-Whitworth's 58 Shop met in a first round tie at St. James's Park. 58 Shop showed a greater knowledge of the game, and won the tie by a comfortable 3-0 margin with goals from Leighley, Gallagher and Charlton.

Hood Haggie's team from Willington Quay played Palmers at Wallsend on 23rd November 1918, Palmers winning 4-0. On the same day Armstrongs-Whitworth's 43 Shop met the NUT Motor Company at Durham City in aid of the Durham branch of Comrades of the Great War. Millie Brannen scored twice for NUT, and Doris Noddhams once for 43 Shop. The report stated that 43 Shop would now meet Blyth Spartans in the next round.

Foster, Blackett & Wilson. played the delightfully-named Dainty Dinahs at Murray Park, Stanley, on 30th November 1918. The Dainty Dinahs were employed at Horners toffee factory in Chester-le-Street, and took their name from the company's most popular brand. They may have been dainty, but they were no match for the team from Foster Blackett, who defeated them 4-0 with goals from Maggie Scott (3) and Maggie Blake.

Round 2 ties:

For the second year running Dorman, Long & Co. found themselves drawn against Richardson, Westgarth. They met at Linthorpe Road, Middlesbrough, on 9th November 1918, and a goalless draw was the result. It appeared they were getting set to restage their previous year's marathon first-round tie, which had taken four meetings to resolve. The replay took place at Samuelson's ground, West Lane, Newport, on 16th November 1918. The result was not reported, but Dorman's appeared in the next round, so we may surmise that they emerged the winners.

On 16th November 1918 Armstrong-Whitworth's 58 Shop were scheduled to meet North East Marine at St. James's Park, but owing to influenza only two members of the 58 Shop team were fit to play. A sizeable crowd had gathered to watch the game, which was in aid of charity, and to paraphrase an old saying "the show had to go on." This was accomplished by splitting the 58 Shop team into two sides - the "Greys" and the "Black and Whites", and with the aid of six munitionettes from amongst the spectators a nine-a-side game was staged. The Greys won by 5 goals to one, the scorers being Potts and Hutchinson of Haggies (2), and Bella Carrott of NEM (2) for the Greys, with Ethel Wallace of 58 Shop getting the solitary goal for the Black and Whites.

On 23rd November 1918 Ashmore, Benson, Pease & Co. of Stockton made their Cup debut in a second round tie against Smith's Dock (indicating that Ashmore Benson had received a bye in the first round). The game was played at the Victoria Ground, Stockton, in aid of the St Dunstan's Hostel for Blinded Soldiers and Sailors. The result was not reported, but Ashmore Benson subsequently appeared in the next round.

Christopher Brown's Girls did not play their second round tie until 28th December 1918, when they met, and thrashed Darlington Railway Athletic 7-1 at Hartlepool.

As mentioned earlier, it was reported that 43 Shop would meet Blyth Spartans in round 2. It is doubtful whether this match ever took place. Of all the newspapers in the North East, the Blyth News was the most assiduous in reporting on munitionette games, frequently devoting several column inches to the exploits of their local heroines, but the last mention of the team in the columns of this newspaper was on 12th September 1918. Given the nature of the work the team members performed - i.e. handling used shell cases for reclamation, it is possible that their jobs were early casualties of demobilisation, and without the support of their employers the team may simply have folded.

Further evidence of disarray in the organisation of the competition emerged while round 2 was in progress; on 19th November 1918 Francis Taylor, the Munitionettes' Competition secretary, was prosecuted at Middlesbrough Magistrates' Court for failure to provide accounts relating to a number of Entertainments Tax tickets. The magistrates accepted his defence that the tickets were in the hands of the organisation, and that he personally was not in a position to provide a balance sheet, and dismissed the charge.

Round 3 ties:

Ashmore, Benson, Pease & Co. and Dorman, Long & Co. were scheduled to meet on 26th December 1918 in a quarter-final tie at Middlesbrough. Once again, no report of the encounter appeared in the newspapers. In the other quarter-final Brown's met Horden on 2nd February 1919 and according to the North Mail defeated them 1-0, though the report incorrectly referred to this as a semi-final tie.

The Tyneside region quarter-finals received better coverage. Both games were played on 8th February 1919. At St. James's Park, Palmer's of Jarrow took on Armstrong-Whitworth's 58 Shop. Palmer's line-up included the formidable Bella Reay, her inclusion proving a wise move. She scored twice before the interval, Beattie Taylor adding a third, with a single goal from 58 Shop's Maggie Short in reply. In the second half Reay got a fourth goal, to make the final score 4-1 in favour of Palmer's.

Armstrong-Whitworth's other team, 60 Shop, were hopelessly hampered in their encounter with Foster, Blackett and Wilson at the Pit Heap ground in Jarrow. They arrived with only 7 players, and had to take the field in this weakened state. Their opponents were awarded two penalties, but on each occasion Foster Blackett's captain, Maggie Scott, failed to capitalise on the opportunity. Eventually Scott scored the only goal of the game from open play to set up a semi-final encounter with their local rivals, Palmer's.

Semi-Finals:

Palmer's and Foster, Blackett met in the Tyneside district semi-final on 1st March 1919. This local derby was played on the Pit Heap ground at Curlew Road, the former home of Jarrow Caledonians F.C. The pitch was in poor condition, and play was on the slow side to begin with. Foster Blackett scored first through Maggie Scott, but the score was levelled when Palmer's were awarded a penalty, which Beattie Taylor converted. In the second half Minnie Seed, formerly with Gosforth Aviation, scored for Palmer's, and then a shot from the same player took a deflection from Hagan, one of the opposing backs, and beat the Foster's keeper. Shortly before the final whistle Wilson scored a second for Foster's but the victory, and a place in the final, belonged to Palmer's.

The Teesside district semi-final was contested between Dorman, Long. and Christopher Brown's. The date of the match is unknown, the only report of the outcome being a brief account in the Northern Daily Mail on 8th March 1919, which stated, "Brown's Girls, by their 6-2 victory over Dorman Long's, have reached the final of the Tyne, Wear and Tees Munitionettes' Cup Competition". The report was clearly referring to an earlier date, as it went on to explain that Brown's were playing a representative side from Middlesbrough on the 8th, and would be without Dorrian, Kirk and McKenna, who were playing at Preston.

The Final:

The final was played on a snow-covered St James's Park on 22nd March 1919. The conditions were atrocious, but despite the weather 10,000 spectators made their way to the ground to witness the match. Both teams included guest players, the line-ups being as follows:

Palmers: Lizzie Greene, A. Malone, Lizzie Gibson, Bella Willis (60 Shop), Lizzie Form (capt.), E. Drinkeld, Beattie Taylor, Elsie Graham, Bella Reay (Blyth Spartans), Mary Lyons, Minnie Seed (Gosforth Aviation)

Brown's: Florrie Holmes, E. Cambridge, Harriet Knight, M. Hodgson, N. Henderson, Nellie Stott (capt.), Mary Dorrian, Nellie Kirk, Winnie McKenna (Bolckow, Vaughan), M. McPherson, E. Ferguson

The scant report of the game which appeared in the Newcastle Journal was, at least, complimentary, praising the teams for putting on a "capital show" despite the wintry weather, and for displaying a sound knowledge of the game. Palmers showed themselves to be the superior team from the kick-off, and a number of glorious chances were engineered by Lyons and Taylor, but, possibly due to the conditions, most of these were badly muffed, the remainder being dealt with by Florrie Holmes in a first-class display of goalkeeping. The interval arrived with the game still goalless. The game changed abruptly immediately after the restart, when Lyons fed Reay with a cross which she fired towards the bottom right-hand corner of the goal. The pace of the shot defeated the unfortunate Holmes, passing under her body into the back of the net. This was the only goal of the game, and it secured the Munitionettes' Cup for Palmer's and a second winner's medal for both Bella Reay and Mary Lyons.

As the munitionettes were laid off, so their football teams were wound up. It is difficult to accurately assess the rate at which munitionette football declined, as the local press lost interest in it after the resumption of the men's professional game. A clue may be gleaned from the accounts of the last two games to be reported in the Newcastle Journal, which were billed as Newcastle Ladies versus Sunderland Ladies. The first took place at Roker Park on 24th May 1919 in aid of the Haverfield Serbian Distress Fund, and the teams lined up as follows:

Sunderland: Holmes, Cambridge, Knight, Henderson, Plummer, Drinkeld, Dorrian, Kirk, McKenna, Seed (capt.), McConnell

Newcastle: Atkinson, Egan, Gibson, Willis (capt.), Short, Form, Taylor, Baine, McGuire, Lyons, Graham

Four members of the Sunderland side (Holmes, Plummer, Dorrian and Kirk) were from Hartlepool, one (McKenna) was from Middlesbrough and one (Drinkeld) was from Jarrow. The Newcastle side was equally cosmopolitan; five members (Egan, Gibson, Form, Taylor and Lyons) were from Jarrow. The event was a success nevertheless; 10,000 spectators turned up to watch the game which Newcastle won 4-1 thanks to a hat-trick from Mary Lyons and a goal from McGuire. Nellie Kirk scored Sunderland's only goal. It was also a success financially, raising £436 for the designated charity.

A return match took place at St. James's Park on 31st May, this time in aid of the Newcastle branch of the St. John's Ambulance Brigade. 9,000 spectators attended, slightly less than at Roker, but the cost of entry was unusually high, ranging from 8d to 2s 4d. The teams were very similar to the previous encounter, except that Sunderland stepped even further outside their catchment area and included two Blyth Spartans players in their squad, Martha O'Brien and Bella Reay. Whether Reay actually played is not known - she was listed as an alternative to Nellie Kirk:

Newcastle: Atkinson, Egan, Gibson, Willis (capt.), Short, Form, Taylor, Graham, McGuire, Lyons, Bains

Sunderland: Holmes, Battista, Knight, Henderson, O'Brien, Plummer, Dorrian, McKenna (South Bank), Reay or Kirk, Seed (capt.), McConnell

Once again the "Newcastle" Ladies proved the stronger, winning this time by 4 goals to nil. Mary Lyons added another goal to her tally, and her Palmers colleague, the six-foot Beattie Taylor, known as "Billy Brawn" because of her style of play, secured a hat-trick.

The composition of these teams suggests that the charity organisers were having to cast their net widely in order to put together attractive teams, which indicates in turn that regular encounters between munitionette teams had all but ceased. From August 1919 a full programme of Football League and minor league games was in operation, and as far as the North East papers were concerned, women's football might never have existed.

Most of the munitionette stars married and settled down to domestic life. Bella Reay, Blyth Spartans' prolific goalscorer, became Mrs William Henstock and in time a proud mother and grandmother. Her life was touched by tragedy however; her husband became one of the first casualties of the Second World War when his ship, the S.S. Lowland, hit a mine off Walton on the Naze in November 1939.

In later life she still enjoyed a game of football, and every Good Friday saw her turn out for the traditional match at Blyth between the Foresters' Arms and the Bebside Inn. A proud and independent individual, she worked for a local farmer until she was in her seventies. One wonders if, while working in the fields, she sometimes cast her eyes in the direction of Croft Park, hearing on the breeze faint echoes of an excited crowd calling out "Howay Bella," and imagining herself, 17 years old again, crashing another fierce drive past a hapless visiting goalkeeper.

Chapter 6
Postscript

Women's football did not die out entirely; although newspaper accounts are rare it is evident that it still flourished in some parts of the country. It remained, however, a vulgar spectacle to the more conservative elements in society, whose influence was greater than their numbers would warrant. A battalion of so-called "Medical Experts" came forward to denounce the game as being potentially injurious to women's health, while others attacked women footballers on the grounds that they were "unladylike". Their ranks even included some feminists, such as Dr. Ethel Williams, the first female doctor to practice in Newcastle upon Tyne, who in her youth had been a suffragette and had taken part in the famous "Mud March" of 1907. The feminist writer Madame Sarah Grand (real name Frances Bellenden Clarke) went into some detail in giving her objections; she condemned lacrosse, football, cricket and some forms of gymnastics as positively injurious, stating "the football-playing girl, the boxing girl, the girl who by gymnastics and physical drill of the too strenuous type, flattens her chest and hardens her muscles will never be the ideal." These misguided opinions were seized upon and eagerly propagated by others who were opposed in principle to the struggle for women's rights.

The North East was not one of the areas in which the female game prospered during this period. Throughout the whole of 1920 the Daily Chronicle, which carried a regular Wednesday column devoted to woman's sport, frequently discussed golf, tennis, swimming, badminton and croquet, but the only mention of women's football, on 25th August, was to state, "You cannot take a game seriously which caused spectators to laugh until they cried."

Nevertheless, activities elsewhere in the country did not go entirely unnoticed, to judge by a report in the Evening Chronicle on 15th January 1921; "Ladies' football, which we never appreciated, is going strong in the Preston area. The team of females connected with some works there have raised £15,000 for charity in the last four and a half years."

This was a reference to the Dick, Kerr team of Preston, which had by now established a formidable reputation. On Boxing Day 1920 they defeated St Helen's Ladies 4-0 at Goodison Park, attracting a crowd of some 53,000, which is still the U.K. record attendance for a women's football match.

The game experienced a brief resurgence at grass roots level during the miners' strike of 1921. Following the return of the coal mines from Government control, the coal owners had sought to reduce miners' wages. A nationwide strike, or lock-out, depending upon one's political viewpoint, was the outcome. The action by the miners was particularly strong in the North East. Women's football, an essentially working-class phenomenon, which had been so successful in fund raising during the Great War, now turned to fund raising on behalf of the miners' families.

An interesting fixture was played at Sherburn Hill, Durham, on 7th May 1921, when the Soup Canteen Ladies were defeated 3-1 by the "Busty Ladies", thanks to a hat-trick by Minnie Dixon. Lest there be any doubt, the team was named after a local coal seam, rather than the physical attributes of the players. A good crowd was in attendance, and a large collection was raised.

The following Monday two women's teams from Scotswood and Newburn met at Towneley Park, Blaydon, and, inspired by this event, a women's team was formed in Blaydon itself. Their first game, against Scotswood Ladies on 23rd May 1921, raised £15 15s 3d in donations. It was an interesting encounter; Blaydon lost 5-0, despite their keeper saving four penalties!

The formation of this team resulted in a particularly virulent attack being published in the Blaydon Courier on 11th June 1921, in the form of a supposed open letter to a lady footballer from her elder sister. Readers may form their own conclusions as to how convincing this is.

Dear Sister,
You ask what I think about you having joined the Ladies Football Club. Not much, and yet a lot. That may sound paradoxical, but allow me to explain. I blush with shame when I picture you, gentle Jennie, my youngest sister, in the habiliments of a football player. You cannot be the shy, blushing sister I remember of ten years ago, when you would have coloured at finding a hole in your stocking. You must have put on the brass since then, and if it really be true that you have developed into a "lady" footballer, then there must be sufficient brass in your face by this time to make a fender. You were never a smart figure - I always got lost in your corsets - and you must certainly be a true example of the ludicrous when clad in your football togs. Think, gentle Jennie, what it would mean if a stitch or two gave way when you bumped the ground? Another reputation would be gone.
What fit of mental aberration has prompted you to become a "lady" footballer? Is there something in the game that appeals to the feminine instinct, or are you out for exercise? Surely, you cannot be seeking exercise - although I admit you would be better without some of your surplus fat - because whenever Mother asked you to dry the dishes you always had some excuse. Then whatever is there in this leather chasing that induces you to don men's garments and parade yourself before hundreds of watery eyes and gaping mouths?

You mention something about the sacred cause of charity. Is charity the only thing that is sacred? Is there not a beautiful flower called modesty? Have you no respect for your sex? Dear, gentle Jennie, are you not aware that every time you enter the dressing room and discard your feminine attire for a pair of men's football knickers and a sweater you not only disgrace yourself, but lower your sex in the eyes of everyone with a sense of decency. Oh, my poor misguided sister, you have degenerated. And what an ass you must make of yourself when kicking and chasing a football, you panting and perspiring little fool. What is this you say in your letter, ".... and we all chew spearmint." Try baccy the next time, it is more appropriate. Oh you horrid wretch. It's enough to make our dear dead grandmother of sacred memory turn in her grave.
But you are still my sister Jennie, and I forgive you your little fling "in the sacred name of charity." Try knitting jumpers.

Believe me,
Your affectionate sister
NORA

Nora, whoever she (or he) may have been, was evidently concerned to get this spiteful piece of vituperation across to as wide an audience as possible, as an identical letter was published in the Consett Guardian on 17th June.

An equally outrageous attack was reported in the Sunderland Echo on 29th June. Brigadier-General Arthur Lloyd, speaking at the AGM of the Royal Salop Infirmary in Shrewsbury, criticised women's football, stating, "I am not a killjoy, but I do say for Heaven's sake do not let ladies degrade themselves by playing football, which is not a ladies' game, and makes fools of them." What triggered his outburst was an announcement from the Treasurer that the hospital had received £300 from the proceeds of a match played at Shrewsbury by women from St Helen's and Chorley. One can well imagine the disappointment of the players at the form of thanks they received.

Despite such attacks, the women continued playing to raise money in support of their men. Their activities were mirrored elsewhere in the region; for example the women of Dipton and Tanfield met twice to determine who would be local top dogs, Tanfield emerging as the victors. On Wearside an attempt was made to recapture the spirit of the Munitionettes' Cup; a trophy, the Wearside and District Ladies Challenge Cup, was presented by Mr Frank Bloom, but it failed to attract more than a handful of entries. The eventual winners were

Silksworth Ladies, who had defeated Felling Ladies 6-0 in the first round, Wearmouth Ladies 3-1 in the second round, and Washington Ladies 2-1 in the semi-final. The final was not reported, and a final may not even have taken place, as only the Silksworth team attended the Cup presentation ceremony on 27th August, when medals were presented to eleven team members, seven reserves and two female trainers. The team, S. Wofendale, Jennie Straughan, Beattie Shillito, L. Kirton, Jennie Foster, Agnes Shillaw, Esther James, Florrie Arkley, Jennie Brown, Maud Cartledge and Eve Shillito raised £72 for local Distress Funds during the course of their brief existence.

Northumberland women also took to the field, and a second Bella Reay emerged in the form of 14 year old Lillian Ritchie of Barrington Colliery, who scored 45 goals in her team's record run of 24 games played with 23 victories. The only side they failed to beat was a reunited Blyth Spartans, captained by Bella herself and including many of her wartime colleagues. Honour was preserved all-round, the game ending in a 0-0 draw thus allowing both teams to preserve their unbeaten records.

If it had only been a matter of village teams raising the odd few pounds, the employers would not have been unduly worried, but crowds of thousands were being attracted to similar games at Football League grounds. For example, a match at Horsley Hill, South Shields, on 10th May 1921 saw a large crowd in attendance to watch Tyneside Ladies defeat Chorley Ladies 6-0, with goals from Lyons (4), Kirk and Dorrian. Three days later an even bigger crowd, some 18,000 in number, saw a North East Coast team take on the Dick, Kerr ladies at Ayresome Park, losing 3-1 to the Preston side.

One organisation which was decidedly concerned about these developments was the Football Association. On the 5th December 1921 it adopted the following drastic resolution:

"Complaints having been made as to football being played by women, the council feel impelled to express their strong opinion that the game of football is quite unsuitable for females and ought not to be encouraged.

Complaints have also been made as to the conditions under which some of these matches have been arranged and played, and the appropriation of receipts to other than charitable objects.

The council are further of the opinion that an excessive proportion of the receipts are absorbed in expenses and an inadequate percentage devoted to charitable objects.

For these reasons the council request clubs belonging to the association to refuse the use of their grounds for such matches."

This ban on the use of F.A. affiliated grounds remained in force until July 1971, and stifled the development of women's football for half a century. In the days following the F.A.'s decision the debate for and against women's football was well-aired in the Press, with several well-known personalities giving their opinions. Among those to speak up for women footballers were the film actress Phyllis Monkman, the teacher and social campaigner Selina Dix, Florence Underwood, Secretary of the British Women's Freedom League, and the anti-vivisectionist and former suffragette Louise Lind-af-Hageby. Jonathan Ridley, for many years President of the Northumberland F.A. and a firm supporter of Blyth Spartans Ladies during the war, had died on 24th August 1921, and one can only speculate as to what stance he might have taken at this time.

Ranged against the women were a motley crowd of reactionaries, including Frank Watts, Manager of Newcastle United, T.W. Bell, Secretary of the Northumberland F.A., J. Weldon, Dean of Durham, George Robey, a popular comedian, Dr Mary Scharlieb, one of the first women doctors in the country, and Eustace Miles, a former world tennis champion and Olympic medallist. A statement attributed to the latter is typical of the shallow level of the objections raised by the "antis". "The kicking is too jerky a movement for women," he stated, "and the strain is likely to be rather severe."

The opposition from Newcastle United was rather ironic; during 1917-1919 munitionette teams had played more than 26 matches at St. James's Park, bringing in much-needed revenue to the club at a time when it was only able to field a junior team, known as Newcastle United Swifts, in the Newcastle and District United League.

A number of reasons have been put forward to explain the F.A's action. One school of thought holds that the popularity of women's football was viewed as a threat to the men's game. It is hard to take this assertion seriously; the number of women's games taking place was small in comparison to the number of men's games, even at the height of the war, and once peacetime conditions had returned the proportion became tiny. However, there were influential voices within society which opposed women's football on the grounds that it was unfeminine. Some, such as the elderly former suffragettes, probably genuinely believed this, but for the male critics it was a convenient smokescreen for their general opposition to the advancement of women's rights.

On the financial side, the proceeds from games were not audited, and this too gave scope for mud-slinging from those opposed to the women's game. Finally, the raising of money for striking workers would have created enemies among a powerful and influential sector of society - the coal owners. There was, perhaps, no single reason, but rather a combination of all these factors which led the to F.A. to its decision.

The response from the women footballers was initially one of defiance. On 12th December 1921 it was announced that an English Women's Football

Association was to be formed. Mr. W. Henley, of Grimsby, was acting Secretary, and representatives of 60 clubs had agreed to attend an inaugural conference in Liverpool. It was their intention to play on, using Rugby grounds if necessary.

During 1922 attempts were made to place the new association on a more commercial footing, a necessary step if it were indeed to become a female equivalent to the Football Association, regulating the women's game throughout the country. A company named the "English Ladies' Football Association Limited" was formed in June, its primary object being "To acquire and take over as a going concern the assets, contracts and liabilities of the Unregistered Association or Club now known as The English Ladies Football Association." Four of the five directors came from Stoke-on-Trent and district, and one from Fleetwood.

The company was formally registered on 27th October, but subsequently filed no annual accounts, nor documents relating to the proposed takeover, and it appears to have remained nothing more than a shell. On 22nd December 1931 a notice appeared in the London Gazette to the effect that it had been struck off the Register of Companies and formally dissolved.

The English Ladies' Football Association was almost certainly doomed from the start; there was no movement towards professionalism within the women's game, and without this, there was never a need for the sort of rigid structures which had evolved within the F.A. and its affiliated leagues .

How long the association continued in existence, and whether it had much of an influence upon the development of women's football in general is unknown. As far as north east England is concerned it seems to have had no impact whatever. In this region some women's teams continued to exist, but no formal league or other tournament structures emerged, and such games as did take place appear to have been relatively infrequent, and organised in support of charitable causes. A good example is the series of Good Friday matches which took place in Darlington in support of the National Union of Railwaymen's Orphans' Fund. This regular fixture commenced in 1928 with a match between Darlington and Windlestone. In 1931 the Darlington Quaker Girls and the Darlington Red Caps took over from the original protagonists, and then in 1933 the fixture settled down to an annual contest between the Quaker Girls and a team drawn from Terry's chocolate factory in York. The final game in the series took place in 1939 between Terry's and Stockton Nomads, the Quaker Girls having disbanded. Several of the games were filmed by Pathe News, and the quality of football shown in these records demonstrates clearly that the participants could not have been playing on a regular basis.

Sources:

1. Newcastle Journal, North Mail, Evening Chronicle, Newcastle Daily Chronicle, Sporting Man, Illustrated Chronicle - Newcastle upon Tyne Central Library.
2. Northern Echo, Blaydon Courier, Chester-le-Street Chronicle, Consett and Stanley Chronicle - Gateshead Central Library.
3. Evening Despatch - Darlington Central Library
4. Stockton and Thornaby Herald - Stockton Central Library
5. North-Eastern Daily Gazette, South Bank Express - Middlesbrough Central Library.
6. Middlesbrough Herald - Redcar Central Library
7. North East Daily Mail - Hartlepool Central Library
8. Shields Gazette - South Shields Central Library
9. Shields Daily News - North Shields Central Library
10. Hexham Courant - Hexham Library
11. Carlisle Journal, Cumberland News – Carlisle Library
12. Belfast Evening Telegraph - The British Library Newspaper Archives
13. North West Evening Mail, Barrow News - Cumbria Record Office
14. Lancashire Daily Post - Harris Library, Preston
15. The Tom Marshall archive – Gateshead Central Library

General References

1. "In A League Of Their Own"' - history of the Dick, Kerr Ladies' Football Team by Gail J. Newsham; published by Scarlet Press 1997, ISBN 1857270290
2. "The Dick, Kerr's Ladies" by Barbara Jacobs; published by Constable and Robinson 2004, ISBN 1841198285
3. "Belles of the Ball" by David J. Williamson; published by R & D Associates 1991, ISBN 0951751204
4. "Women at War 1914-1918" by Arthur Marwick; published by Fontana Paperbacks 1977, ISBN 0006344968
5. "Women's Factory Work in WW1" by Gareth Griffiths; published by Alan Smith 1991, ISBN 086299795X
6. "On Her Their Lives Depend" - a history of female munitions workers in the Great War by Angela Woollacott; published by the University of California Press 1994, ISBN 0520085027
7. "A Game for Rough Girls? " by Jean Williams; published by Routledge 2003, ISBN 0415263387
8. "1914-1918 - The History of the First World War" by David Stevenson; published by Penguin Books 2004, ISBN 0140268170

Wheatley Hill Ladies Football Team 1909
Meggy Lowther, Lizzy Luke, ?, Meggy Farrow, Lizzy Champley, Meggy Philips, Bella Cowie (kneeling)

Wheatley Hill Rosy Rapids in 1909

The Rosy Rapids may have been the first women's football team in the region

(Wheatley Hill Local History Club)

Armstrong Whitworth & Co. Munitionettes at St. James's Park - 21st April, 1917

The two ladies at the back wearing badges in their hats are members of the Women's Police Service

(from "Ryhope and Silksworth" by J. N. Pace and Andrew Clark, Tempus Publishing 2006)

When teams of women and men met on the field the men were expected to play with their hands tied behind their backs. The picture above shows Haslemere Ladies playing the Seaforth Reserves in June 1917

Blyth Spartans - Munitionette Cup Winners 1918
back row: Hannah Weir, Lizzie James, Nellie Fairless
centre row: Agnes Sample, Martha O'Brien, Bella Metcalfe
front row: Dollie Allen, Annie Allen, Bella Reay, Ada Reed, Jennie Morgan
(photograph courtesy of John Morgan)

Bolckow, Vaughan & Co. Munitionettes

Munitionette Cup Finalists 1918

back: Emily Milner, Amelia Farrell, Greta Kirk, Violet Sharples

front: Elizabeth Powell, Mary Mohan, Mercy Page, Winnie McKenna, Gladys Reece, Olive Percival, Annie Wharton

(photograph courtesy of Peter McNaughton)

Munitionettes' Cup - Winners' medal presented to Jennie Morgan

(photograph courtesy of John Morgan)

Palmer's Munitionettes - Munitionette Cup Winners 1919

back row: Mrs. Ornsby (Female Supervisor), Christiana Connon, Susannah Connon, Lizzie Form
front row: unknown, unknown, Mary Lyons, unknown, Beattie Taylor

(photograph courtesy of the Imperial War Museum - image Q11074)

Christopher Brown's Munitionettes - Munitionette Cup Finalists 1919

back row: M. Hodgson, E. Cambridge, G. Kelley, M. McKenzie (at rear), N. Henderson, Harriet Knight, Matilda Booth,
front row: Mary Dorrian, Norah Murray, Nellie Stott, M. McPherson, E. Ferguson

(photograph courtesy of Keith Hewitson)

BELLA WINS THE CUP FOR PALMERS.

The winning (and only) goal of the match scored by Bella Reay (Palmers).

How the Newcastle 'Illustrated Chronicle' reported Palmer's Victory in the Cup

Bella Reay - Blyth Spartans and England

An inscription on the rear of the photograph in Bella's own hand reads "Bella Reay, aged 17, in Blyth Ladies Spartans Team. Trained by Navy Lads whose boat was in Blyth harbour"

(photograph courtesy of Yvonne Crawford)

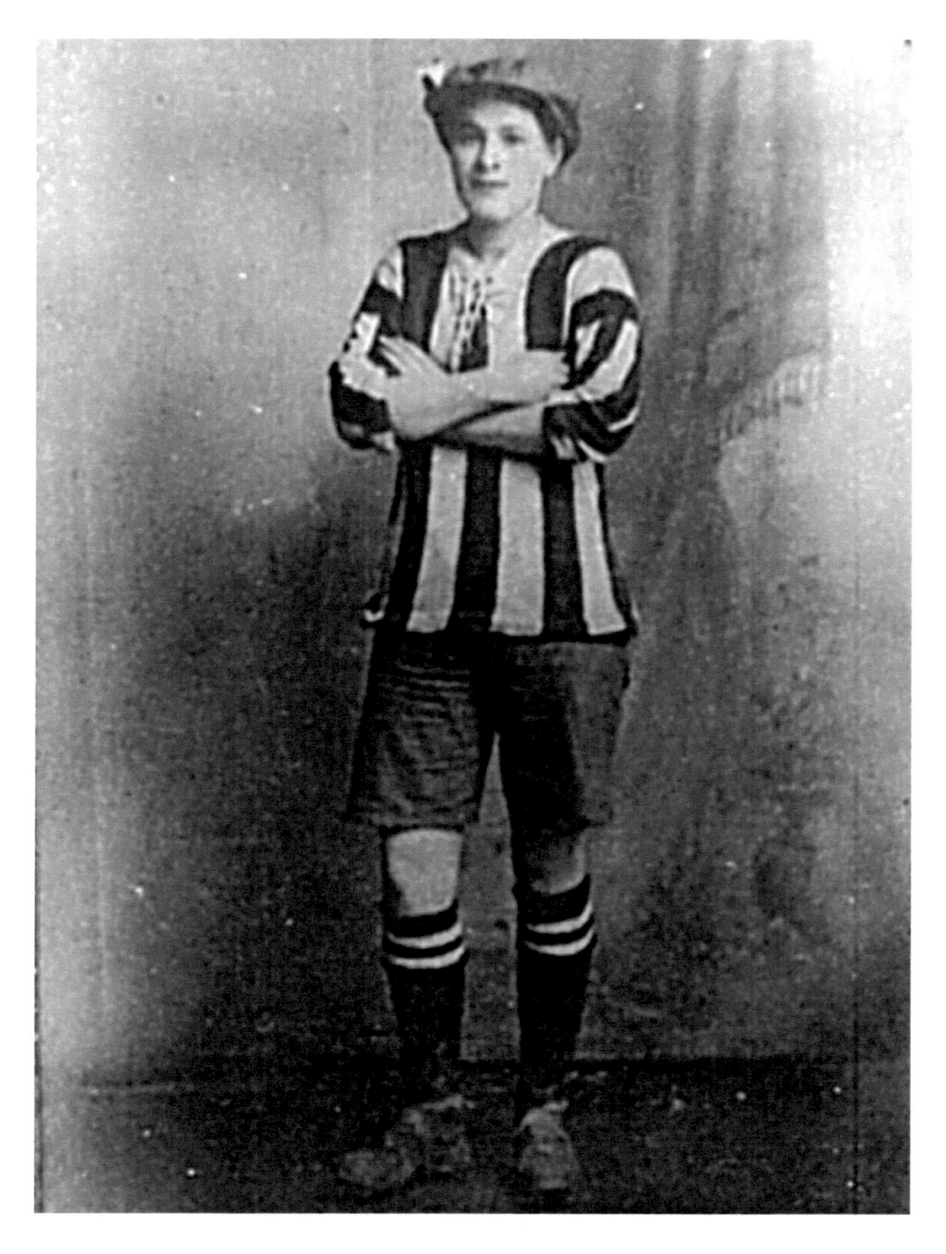

Maggie Scott - Palmers and England

An all-round sportswoman, Maggie took part in a boxing match in Jarrow, swam the River Tyne for a bet, and at the age of 70 was captain of a ladies' darts team

(photograph courtesy of Winnie Brass)

Mary Lyons - Palmers and England

Palmer's star inside-forward and a prolific goalscorer, Mary was only 14 years old when she made her debut in an international match

Mary Dorrian - Christopher Brown's and England
A winger with terrific pace, Mary both made and scored goals

The Minister of Labour (anxious to find work for the ex-munitionette drawing unemployment pay).
"HERE, MODOM, IS A CHARMING MODEL WHICH WOULD SUIT YOU, IF I MAY SO PUT IT, DOWN TO THE GROUND."

After the war it was expected that the munitionettes would return to domestic service - an occupation that most of them detested

(Punch Magazine - May 1919)

Appendix 1

This is a compilation of 268 munitionette matches played between December 1916 and May 1919. In many cases only minimal details appeared in the local press, and on some occasions the score was not reported. They are listed as reported, complete with spelling errors.

1916-12-26 *Hawthorn Leslie's Women 6 - Hawthorn Leslie's Men 2*
Played at the Hebburn Argyle ground in aid of the Soldiers and Sailors Fund.
Scorers: Dunning (4), Foley, Davidson for the women, Tafferty and Watson for the men, who played in "comic costumes."

1917-02-03 *Wallsend Slipway 0 - North Eastern Marine 3*
Played at Wallsend before 2,000 spectators in aid of the Wallsend Branch of the Queen Mary Needlework Guild. The game was refereed by Bill McCracken of Newcastle United.
Scorers: Carrott (pen), Bolland, Jackson

1917-03-10 *North Eastern Marine 4 - Swan & Hunter's 2*
Played at Wallsend AFC ground before 2,000 spectators in aid of the Wallsend Heroes' Fund and Wallsend Motor Ambulance Fund.
Scorers: Scott (2) and Jackson (2) for NEM, Mason and Elvin (pen) for Swan Hunter.

1917-03-31 *Blaydon Park Villa 6 - Lady Munition Workers 4*
Women versus Men comic football match; the teams met at Cochrane Street and marched to the ground at Blaydon Haughs.

1917-04-05 *Foster Blackett & Wilson's Ladies 1 - Armstrongs Naval Yard 0*
At Hebburn Colliery, in aid of Aged Miners' Homes.

1917-04-07 *North-Eastern Marine 3 - Wallsend Slipway 1*
Played at Hawkey's Lane, North Shields, in aid of the Y.M.C.A. Sports Committee; refereed by Bill McCracken.

1917-04-09 *Expanded Metal Co. Munition Girls 1 - Central Marine Munition Girls 0*
Played at the Victoria Ground, Hartlepool before 4,000 spectators in aid of Yorkshire Prisoners of War. This was the first munition girls' match at Hartlepool
Scorer: Caine
Central Marine: N. Smith, May Seal, J. Burns, Jennie Leighton, Maud Rutter, L. Tyson, Mabel Campbell, Amy King, Florrie Norris, Mary Wilkinson, Hilda Allan
Expansion: Stevenson, Abbey, N. Relton, Spenceley, Barnett, Relton, Plummer, M. Stevenson, Caine, Agar, Foxton.

1917-04-21 *Wallsend Slipway Women Workers 1 - North East Marine 1*
Played at St James's Park in aid of Joseph and Jane Cowen Training Home, Benwell.

1917-04-21 *Armstrongs (Elswick) 4 - Wallsend Naval Yard 2*
Played at St James's Park in aid of Joseph and Jane Cowen Training Home, Benwell.

1917-04-28 *Expansion 1 - Central Marine 0*
Played at Caledonian Road, Hartlepool before 3,000 spectators
Scorer: Harriet Agar
Expansion: Edie Stevenson, Becca Abbey, Mary Relton, Bella Plummer, Jessie Spenceley, Norah Barnett, Lizzie Kane (capt.), Annie Relton, Harriet Agar, Martha Stevenson, Mary Atkinson
Central Marine: E. Mailen, May Seal (capt.), Nellie Smith, Jennie Leighton, Susan Cavanagh, E. Tyson, Amy King, Violet Griffiths, Agnes Harvey, Florrie Norris, Doris Lowcock.

1917-04-30 *Wallsend Slipway v North East Marine Engineering Works*
Played at St James's Park in aid of Dr Barnardo's Homes
Slipway: N Horne, G Timbers, A Yeaman, S Matthews, M Short, B Turnbull, M Irwin, M Gray, M Mulligan, V Bryant, L McConnell
N.E.M: M Watson, M Smith, N Aitkin, B Holloran, B Carrott, C McCann, L Scott, N Weygood, B Jackson, D Wallace, M Catterick.

1917-05-12 *Palmers Female Munition Workers 0 - Armstrong Naval Yard Female Munition Workers 2*
Played at Jarrow before 2,000 spectators in aid of the local branch of the Queen Mary Needlework Guild. (this was Palmers' first game - after only 3 practice matches). The game raised £76 6s. 6d.
Scorers: Ina Wardhaugh, Bella Thompson.

1917-05-12 *Expanded Metal Works 3 - Christopher Brown Ltd. 0*
Played at West Hartlepool, raising £22 in aid of the Hull Sailors' Orphans Home.

1917-05-12 *Wallsend Slipway 0 - North East Marine 2*

Played at Horsley Hill, South Shields, before 5,000 spectators, in aid of the Tyne Interned Seamen's Fund, raising approximately £140.

Scorers: Wallace, Garrett*

NEM: Doich, Fleck, Miller, Holohan, Garrett* (capt.), McCarron, Weygood, Wallace, Atkin, Scott, Jackson

Slipway: Horne, Chambers, Holmes, Gray, Short, Yeaman, Quinn, Turnbull (capt.), Bryant, McConnell, Mulligan

* this should read Carrott

1917-05-19 *Central Marine Munition Girls 2 - Brown's Munition Girls 2*

Played at the Victoria Ground, West Hartlepool in aid of the Durham Aged Miners' Homes.

Scorers: Kirk (2 pen) for Brown's; A. King, A Harvey for Central Marine

Brown's (blue and white): D Watt, N Henderson, E Cambridge, E Herd, G Kelley, E Snowball, M Dorrian, N Kirk, N Stott, A Cusworth, E Ferguson.

1917-05-26 *Brown's Saw Mill v United Shipyard Munition Girls*

Shipyard United: Phillips, Russell, Winspear, Johnson, Richards, Addison, Forsythe, Dorkin, Coverdale, Mason, Golding

Brown's: D. Watt, Henderson, Cambridge, Herd, Kelley, McKenzie, Dorrian, Kirk, Stott, Murray, Ferguson.

1917-05-26 *Wallsend Slipway & Engineering Company 0 - North Eastern Marine Engineering Works 4*

Played at Coxlodge Colliery field in aid of the Northumberland War Hospital, Gosforth

Scorers: Bella Carrott, Ethel Jackson (3)

Slipway: Maggie Short, Grace Chambers, Mrs Grey, Blanche Lacey, Maggie Thompson, Eva Harding, Mary McGregor, Bella Turnbull, Mrs Queen, Miss Maconnel, Violet Bryant

N.E.M: Bella Carrott, Hilda Weygood, Miss M Doeck, E Catterick, Florry Rothwell, Bridget Hollaran, Mary Atkin, E Scott, Ethel Jackson, Annie McCarron, Florry Wallace

Scorers: Ethel Jackson (3), Maggie Short.

1917-05-26 *Birtley Shell Shop Girls 0 - Birtley Cartridge Case Girls 5*
Played at the Cricket Club, Chester-le-Street before 1,000 spectators in aid of the Chester-le-Street Heroes' Fund
Scorers: N. Clarke (2), L. Marsh (2), Matthews (pen)
Shell Shop (blue): M. Drennan, E. Chapman, N. Belton, L. Dent, N. Lonsdale, M. Pearson, D. Little, M. Atlass, L. Laverick, L. Mitchell, A. Keen
Cartridge Case Shop (pink): M. Gascoine, J. Arkless, J. Turnbull, N. Clarke, A. Churcher, E. Earley, L. Herdman, J. Marsh, S. Matthews, L. Marsh, M. Liddle

1917-06-09 *North East Marine 2 - Wallsend Slipway 0*
Played at Horsley Hill, South Shields in aid of the Sailors' Day Fund
Scorer: Ethel Jackson (2)
NEM: Doich, Fleck, Miller, Holohan, Garrett* (capt.), McCarron, Weygood, Wallace, Atkin, Scott, Jackson
Slipway: Horne, Chambers, Holmes, Gray, Short, Yeaman, Quinn, Turnbull (capt.), Byrant, McConnell, Mulligan
* this should read Carrott.

1917-06-09 *Brown's Munition Girls 2 - Central Marine Girls 1*
Played at Murton in aid of the Hesleden Aged Miners' Treat Fund
Scorers: Norah Murray, Nellie Kirk for Brown's; Florrie Norris (pen) for Central Marine
Brown's: (from) Watt, Henderson, Cambridge, Herd, Kelley, Snowball, Dorrian, Stott, Murray, Kirk, Ferguson, Cusworth, McKenzie

1917-06-09 *Birtley Cartridge Case Girls 2 - Birtley Cartridge Case Fitters 3*
Women v Men Costume match played at the Cricket Pitch, Chester-le-Street in aid of the Chester-le-Street Heroes' Fund.
Girls: Gascoine, Archer, Turnbull, Urwin, Marsh, Clewes, Liddle, Churcher, Matthews, Clark, Herdman
Fitters: Fairley, Scrimgeour, Gilties, Brown, Watts, Birkett, Grant, Nicholson, Chipchase, Robson, Gibson.

1917-06-16 *Palmer's Girl Workers 2 - Armstrong Naval Yard Girl Workers 3*
Played at Jarrow, raising £50 in aid of the Jack Cornwell Memorial Homes.

1917-06-23 *Birtley Cartridge Case Girls 3 - North East Marine 3*
Played at the cricket field, Chester-le-Street in aid of the Chester-le-Street Heroes' Fund.

1917-07-07 *Central Marine Engine Works 3 - North Eastern Marine Engine Works 2*
Played at West Hartlepool in connection with the Munition Girls' Sports Day.

1917-07-14 *Palmer's Munition Girls 0 - Wallsend Slipway 4*
Played at Croft Park, Blyth in aid of the Blyth Military Merit and Homecoming Funds. Slipway played in black and white, Palmer's in blue and red.

1917-07-14 *Brown's Munition Girls 2 - Trimdon Girls 1*
Played at the Victoria Ground, West Hartlepool before 1,000 spectators in aid of the British and French Red Cross Societies.
Scorers: Leggart for Trimdon; Murray and Kirk for Brown's.

1917-07-21 *Brown's Munition Girls 1 - Trimdon Grange Girls 0*
Played at Wheatley Hill in aid of the Wheatley Hill Welcome Home Fund. This was the first match of its kind played at Wheatley Hill.
Scorer: L. Kirk (pen)

1917-07-21 *Elswick No 60 Shop 4 - Ryton Girls 3*
Described as a "Novelty Costume football match", and played at Prudhoe Flower Show Ground in aid of the Prudhoe District Soldiers' Welcome Fund.
Scorers: Jenny Russell, Gerty Ions and E. Gallagher for Ryton; Bella Willis (2), Ada Shaw and an own goal for Elswick.
(The Hexham Courant reported the match as 60 Shop and Ryton versus Derwent Haughs)

1917-07-28 *Brown's Munition Girls 13 - Dorman Long Munition Girls 1*
Played at the Victoria Ground, Hartlepool before 500-600 spectators in aid of the Hartlepools Police Court Mission.
Scorers: Nellie Kirk (4), Murray (4), Dorrian (in first half).

1917-08-04 *North East Engineering 3 - Willington Foundry 0*
Played at Murton AFC in front of a good attendance. Mr W. McCracken of Newcastle United refereed.

1917-08-06 *North East Marine 1 - Wallsend Slipway 1*

Played at The Ridings, Hexham, in aid of Hexham Abbey, the Serbian Red Cross and the YMCA. The game was refereed by Will McCracken, who afterwards auctioned the ball, which was purchased for £2 by Marjorie Henderson, Commandant of the Red Cross V.A.D. Hospital in Hexham (and eldest daughter of Charles W. Henderson, owner of The Riding).

1917-08-04 *Blyth Spartans Munition Ladies 7 - Jack Tars 2*

Women versus Men match played at Croft Park.

Scorers: Bella Reay (6), A. Nother

Spartans: L James, M Robertson, H Malone, B Metcalfe (capt.), A Reed, N Fairless, J Nuttall, D Allen, M O'Brien, B Reay, A Sample

Jack Tars: S.P.O. Gibbs, L.S. Guest, S.N. Carmichael, Sig. Frost, A. B. Gray, C. Betty, S.P.O. (T.W.) Reeves, P.O. (S.W.) Reeves, P.O. Baker (capt.), S.P.O. Lawrence, C.C. Gill

1917-08-06 *Trimdon Grange Munition Girls 3 - Hartlepool Marine Engineering Girls 2*

Played at Durham University, raising £50 in aid of the D.L.I. Prisoners of War Fund.

Scorers: Armstrong (2) and Leggett for Trimdon; Arkless and Morris for Hartlepool.

1917-08-18 *Blyth Spartans Munition Ladies 10 - Blyth United Munition Ladies 1*

Played at Croft Park, in aid of the Cowpen and Crofton Workmen's Patriotic Fund.

Scorers: Reay (7), Metcalfe, Nuttall, Allen for Spartans; Downey (pen) for United

Spartans: M. James, N. Fairless, H. Malone, A. Sample, M. O'Brien, B. Metcalfe, J. Nuttall, M. Robinson, B. Reay, D. Allen, A. Read

United: M. Spinks, E. Davison, H. Lawton, M. Foster, J. Watson, F. Thompson, M. Shields, J. Balls, S. Atkinson, H. Harvey, M. Downey.

1917-08-18 *Brown's 8 - Richardson Westgarth's 0*

Played at the Victoria Ground, West Hartlepool, before 500-600 spectators in aid of the Yorkshire Regiment Prisoners of War Fund.

Scorers: M Hodgson (3), N Hamilton (3), Ada Cusworth, E Snowball.

1917-08-18 *Brown's Girls 1 - Military XI 2*

Played after the Brown's versus Richardson, Westgarth game; the Military XI was a team of soldiers who played with their hands tied behind their backs.

1917-08-18 *North East Marine 1 - Palmers 0*

Final of the 5-a-side tournament staged as part of the Angus Sanderson Sports Day at St James's Park. Other teams participating were: Aerodrome Gosforth, NUT Scotswood, Clarke Chapman, Swan Hunters, Angus Sanderson No. 1, Angus Sanderson No. 2.

1917-08-25 *Christopher Brown's Athletics Club 6 - Bolckow, Vaughan's 1*

Played at West Hartlepool in aid of the D.L.I. Prisoners of War Fund.

Scorers: Nellie Kirk (4), Mary Dorrian and Norah Murray for Brown's; Winnie McKenna for Bolckow's.

1917-08-25 *Brown's Girls 5 - 347 Works Company DLI 5*

Women versus Men match played at the same venue on behalf of the same cause as above. The men played with hands tied behind their backs.

Scorers: E. Snowball (2), M. Hodgson (2), A. Allen for the women; Private Williams (2), Sergeant Grange, Lance-Corporal Brown and Private Foster for the men.

1917-09-01 *Palmer's 0 - Wallsend Slipway 2*

Played at the Grange House Field, Morpeth, in aid of the Morpeth V.A.D. Hospital

Scorer: Jackson (2).

1917-09-01 *Brown's No. 1 3 (minors) - Central Marine Engine Works No. 1 0*

The final of a six-a-side tournament played at the Friarage Ground, Hartlepool before 1,500 spectators in aid of the Sailors' Flower Day Fund.

A "minor" was scored when the ball crossed the goal line

between a goal post and a flag placed a few yards outside it.
Brown's: N. McKenzie, E. Hird, N. Stott (capt.), N. Kirk, N. Murray, M. Dorrian.
Central Marine: E. Mallen, M. Seal (capt.), N. Smith, J. Arnell, F. Norris, A. KIng.
The other teams participating were: Brown's No. 2, Central Marine Engine Works No. 2, Richardson, Westgarth's No.1, Richardson, Westgarth's No.2, Shipyard United No. 1, Shipyard United No. 2, Expansion No. 1, Expansion No. 2.

1917-09-08 *Blyth Spartans 6 - Navy 4*
Women versus Men match played at Bedlington in aid of the Soldiers' and Sailors Comforts Fund
Scorers: Reay (4), D. Allen, J. Nuttall.

1917-09-08 *Richardson, Westgarth Munition Girls v Expanded Metal Co. Munition Girls*
Played at Friarage Field, Hartlepool, in aid of Lord Roberts' Workshop for Disabled Soldiers.

1917-09-08 *Brown's 0 - Central Marine Engine Works 1*
Played at West Hartlepool "on behalf of one of Brown's girls who injured her hand some time ago"
Scorer: E. Henderson.

1917-09-08 *Brown's 2 - Wallsend Slipway 0*
Played after the Brown's versus Central Marine match in aid of the same cause
Scorers: N Kirk (pen), Booth.

1917-09-15 *Wallsend Slipway 1 - North East Marine 1*
Played at Bishop Auckland before 2,000 spectators in aid of the local War Honours Fund.

1917-09-15 *Blyth Spartans 5 - Jack Tars 3*
Women v Men match played at Seghill in aid of the Seghill Presentation Fund.
Scorers: Reay (2), Nuttall (2), Fairless.

1917-09-15 *Blyth United Munition Ladies 5 - Military XI 4*
Women versus Men match played at Cramlington
Scorers: M. Burke (2), M. Smith (3) for the ladies.

1917-09-22 *Palmer's Shipbuilding Co. 0 - North-Eastern Marine Engineering 0*

Played at Sunderland Royal Rovers' ground, Hendon, W McCracken referee.

NEM (blue): A. Nelson, F. Wilson, F. Rothwell, H. Weygood, B. Carrot, E. Catterick, M. Wallace, A. McCarron, M. Atkins, E. Scott, E. Jackson

Palmer's (red): E. Form, E. Young, S. Connan, E. Gibson, M. Scott, M. Bainbridge, N. Robertson, M. Todd, E. Graham, M. Stewart, G. Connan

The teams were described as the unbeaten champions of Durham and Northumberland respectively.

1917-09-22 *Blyth Spartans Munitions Girls 0 - Wallsend Slipway Munition Girls 0*

Played at Croft Park to aid the widow and family of Peter Mackin, a local footballer killed in action on Easter Monday.

Spartans: L James, H Malone, N Fairless, A Sample, M O'Brien, B Metcalfe, A Read, H Carnaby, B Reay, D Allan, J Nuttall

Slipway: Horne, Chambers, Short, Grey, Jackson, Mulligan, Turnbull, A McConnell, Clark, Graham, Bryant.

1917-09-27 *Blyth United Munition Ladies 8 - Royal B's 6*

Played at Cambois

Scorers: M. Berg (3), S. Gillespie (2), M. Smith (2), H. Harvey.

1917-09-29 *Birtley 2 - Sacriston 0*

Played at Sacriston in aid of the 'Sacriston' bed in the St John Ambulance Hospital in France.

Scorers: Matthews, Laverick.

1917-09-29 *Wallsend Slipway 2 - Walker Naval Yard 0*

Played at St James's Park before 5,000 spectators in aid of the Royal Victoria Infirmary (raised £157 3s 7d)

Scorer for Slipway: Ethel Jackson (2).

1917-09-29 *Rise Carr Girls 3 - Darlington Railway Athletic 1*
Played at Brinkburn Road, Darlington
Scorers: Hooper (2), Lodge, for Rise Carr; Parkinson for Railway Athletic
Rise Carr: L McGuigan, H Blewett, E Ashton, L Roberts, M Appleton, J Lodge, E Hawkes, D Lythe, L Hooper, A Brittan, L Johnson
Railway Athletic: Brown, Martin, Greenhalgh, Johnson, Kitchin, Carr, Watson, M Atkinson, Peckitt, Parkinson, McLeod.

1917-10-06 *Blyth Spartans Munition Ladies 3 - Palmer's Shipyard Ladies 0*
Played at New Hartley in aid of the local Homecoming and Merit Fund.
Scorers: Reay (3), Allen
Spartans: L James, H Malone, N Fairless, A Sample, M O'Brien, B Metcalfe, A Read, M Lowery, B Reay, D Allan, J Nuttall; Reserves: F Harris, D Summers
Palmer's: M Scott, E Young, E Gibson, H Stewart, S Cannon, N Bainbridge, C Cannon, M Porthouse, E Graham, M Todd, N Robertson; Reserves: E Form, A Fawcus, S McCanlan.

1917-10-06 *Wallsend Slipway Munition Girls 4 - N. E. Marine Girls 0*
Played at Murray Park, West Stanley in aid of the Stanley Flag Day Committee's £1,000 Patriotic Fund for local soldiers and sailors.
Scorer: Bryant (4).
Slipway team: Horne, Chambers, Short, Gray, Mulligan, Turnbull (capt.), Quinn, Clark, Watson, Bryant, McConnell.

1917-10-06 *Bolckow, Vaughan 2 - West Hartlepool Central Marine 0*
Played at South Bank
Scorer: Winnie McKenna (2).

1917-10-06 *Hartlepool Shipper's Union 1 - Trimdon Munitionettes 1*
Played at the Brewery Field, Spennymoor in aid of the Spennymoor Ambulance Association and the Trimdon Grange Welcome Home Fund.
Scorers: Forsyth for Hartlepool, Leggett (pen) for Trimdon.

1917-10-06 *Brown's Mills 0 - Expansion Works 0*
Played at the Victoria Ground, West Hartlepool in aid of the Sailors' Comforts Fund.

1917-10-06 *NER Munition Shop Girls 6 - Wounded Soldiers 7*

Played at Feethams, Darlington in aid of the Soldiers' Comforts Fund; a total of £20 was raised. The soldiers were from the Woodside Hospital, and played with their hands behind them.

Scorers: Watson (2), Peckitt, Atkinson, Kitching and Haddikin for NER; Atkinson (2), Anderson (2), Holloway, Reid, Shirt for the soldiers.

1917-10-06 *Stripes 1 - Whites 1*

Sunderland Ladies' practice match, played at Holmes' Field

A team: A. Grey, Miss English, Mrs Curtis, Miss Drinkeld, B Atkinson, K O'Donell, C Dingnall, H. Walker, L. Crone, Sarah S. Wilson, Mrs H Richmond

B team: F Catchesides, S McCormick, M Reed, S McBride, S Hardy, H Noble, N Tingley, Miss Howarth, Sarah McCormick, M Koltsz, Miss Stephenson.

1917-10-13 *Armstrong-Whitworth 59 Shop 3 - Armstrong-Whitworth 43 Shop 1*

Munition Girls' Cup R1, played at Blaydon Road, Scotswood; proceeds donated to Scotswood Welcome Home Fund

Scorers: E Wallace (2), Ella Fairbairn for 59 Shop, M Dryden for 43 Shop

(Note: 59 Shop was actually 57 Shop).

1917-10-13 *Rise Carr v Darlington Railway Athletic*

Scheduled to be played at Crook in aid of the local Ladies' Sewing Guild

Railway Athletic: Brown, Martin (capt.), Greenhalgh, Parkinson, Blacklock, Carr, Watson, Atkinson, Teckett, Johnson, McLeod; Reserves: Franks, Smith, Habdikin, Pearson, McLeod, Atkinson.

1917-10-13 *Bolckow,Vaughan 1 - Dorman Long (Port Clarence) 1*

Munition Girls' Cup R1, played at Ayresome Park, in aid of the Middlesbrough War Heroes' Fund.

1917-10-13 *Burradon Ladies 1 - Blyth Spartans Munitions Ladies 4*

Played at Burradon in aid of the Burradon Soldiers' and Sailors' Comfort Fund

Scorers: A Read, B Reay, J Nuttall (2) for Spartans, G North for Burradon

Burradon: Mrs Hepsen, L Peace, G North, J Littlefair, M Smith, G Scobie, M Malone, J Connell, G North; Reserves: M Heslop, M A Robson

Blyth Spartans: L James, H Malone, M Fairless, A Sample, M O'Brien, B Metcalfe, A Reid, L Lowery, B Reay, D Allen, J Nuttall; Reserves: F Harris, D Summers.

1917-10-13 *Birtley Munition Girls 2 - Scotswood 60 Shop 1*

Played at Springwell in aid of the Springwell Soldiers' and Sailors' Welcome Fund.

1917-10-13 *Christopher Brown's Munition Workers 4 - Belle Vue Munition Workers 1*

Played in the grounds of Seaham Hall before 1,000 spectators in aid of the Wounded Soldiers of Seaham Hall and District. This was Belle Vue's first match

Scorers: Allen (2), Hodgson, Dorrian for Brown's; Snowball for Belle Vue.

1917-10-20 *Wallsend Slipway Ladies 0 - North-East Marine Ladies 0*

Played at Leadgate Park before 2,000-3,000 spectators in aid of the local War Dependants' Fund. The match raised £72 4s, and after expenses £60 was handed over to the Fund.

Slipway (green and white): M. Horne, G. Chambers, M. Short, M. Gray, M. Mulligan, B. Turnbull (capt.), M. Quinn, L. Clark, V. Bryant, J. Watson, L. McConnell; reserve: A. McConnell

NEM (black and white): A. Nelson, F. Wilson, F. Rothwell E. Catterick, B. Carrott (capt.), H. Weygood, F. Wallace, A. McCarron, E Jackson, M. Atkins, E. Scott; reserve: M. Bruce.

1917-10-20 *Darlington N.E.R. 4 - Stephenson's 1*

Played at Brinkburn Road, Darlington before only a sprinkling of spectators. Stephenson's had only 10 players.

Scorers: McLeod (2), Peckitt and Martin for N.E.R.; Worcester for Stephenson's.

1917-10-20 *Blyth Spartans v Aviation Girls*

Munitions Girls' Cup R1, scheduled to be played at New Hartley in aid of the Sailors' Orphans' Home. This game was postponed at the last minute owing to the military authorities refusing to sanction it.

Blyth (from): Lizzie James, Hannah Malone, Nellie Fairless, Agnes Sample, Martha O'Brien, Bella Metcalfe, Ada Read, Lizzie Lowery, Bella Reay, Dolly Allen, Jean Nuttall, Jean Morgan, Dolly Turner, Florrie Harris

Aviation (from): Florence Benson, Florence Tweddle, Ada Simms, Emma Waters, Maud Best, Ethel Young, Emily Erwin, Lizzie Spedding, Dolly Connelly, Minnie Seed, Sylvia Mansfield, Maggie Carr.

1917-10-27 *Palmer's 0 - Birtley Cartridge Case Factory 0*

Munition Girls' Cup R1, played at Bishop Auckland in aid of the Sailors' Orphans Home Scheme.

Palmer's (from): M Scott, E Young, E Gibson, H Stewart, S Connon, M Bainbridge, C Connon, M Porthouse, E Graham, M Todd, N Robinson, E Form, A Fawcus, L McCaulay.

1917-10-27 *Armstrong Whitworth No. 60 Shell Shop 2 - Wallsend Slipway 0*

Munition Girls' Cup R1, played at Blaydon Road, Scotswood in aid of the Discharged Soldiers' and Sailors' Federation. scorer: Bella Willis (2)

Armstrong's: Nance Murdock, Alice Hinson, Elizabeth Ramshaw, Maggie Cooper, Frances Lister, Jessie Dickinson, Florence Taylor, Elsie Gardner, Gertie Ions, Grace Battista, Ada Shaw, Charlotte Irving, Elizabeth Wynn, Lizzie Gallagher, Isabella Willis

Slipway: Margaret Stevenson, May Horne, Eva Harding, Agnes McConnell, Isabella Turnbull, Mary Mulligan, M Quinn, Isabella Arthur, May Gray, Isabella Turner, Elizabeth McConnell, Jane Watson, Maggie Short, Grace Chambers, Elizabeth Clark, Violet Bryant, May Fleck, Margaret Hayton .

1917-10-27 *North-East Marine 3 - N.U.T (South Benwell) 0*
Munition Girls' Cup R1, played at Hawkeys' Lane in aid of the widow and family of the late secretary of North Shields YMCA.

1917-10-27 *Bolckow, Vaughan 2 - Dorman Long (Port Clarence) 1*
Munition Girls' Cup R1 (replay), played at South Bank in aid of the Red Cross and Soldiers' Parcel Fund.
Bolckow, Vaughan (from): R. Murphy, J. Martin, G. Kirk, A. Farrel, E. Milner, L. Powell, A. Floyd, E. Crier, W. McKenna (capt.), A. Wharton, A. Leach
Dorman Long (from): A. Briggs (capt.), M. Robinson, L. Robson, J. Clay, R. Boyle, N. Fewster, A. White, A. Hardman, A. Taylor, A. McIntyre, L. Donnelly, L. Gallagher, H. Taylor.

1917-10-27 *Morpeth Post Office Girls 0 - Blyth Spartans 3*
Played at Morpeth in aid of the Morpeth Cottage Hospital and War Heroes Funds.
Scorers: A. Read, B. Reay (2)
Spartans: L James, H Malone, N Fairless, A Sample, B Metcalfe, M O'Brien, A Read, L Lowery, B Reay, F Harris, J Morgan; reserves: D Summers, A Allen.
Morpeth: M Mackey, M Lowes, J Potts, P Kelly, A West, M Brown, A Henry, M Hindmarsh, M Wade, D Cairns, A Wood.

1917-10-27 *Gosforth Aviation v Armstrong's Naval Yard*
Played at Hendon
Naval Yard: Heron, Hutchinson, Patton, Lister, Nendick, Jane, Thompson, Wardaugh, Scott, Ruddock.

1917-10-27 *Belle Vue Munition Girls 1 - Brown's Munition Girls 3*
Played at Sherburn Hill in aid of the village War Working Party
Scorer: M. Dorrian, N. Murray (2) for Browns; Ada Cusworth for Belle Vue.

1917-11-03 *Blyth Spartans Ladies 1 - Wallsend Slipway Ladies 1*
Played at Seaton Delaval in aid of the R.A.O.B. War Memorial Fund. Scorer for Spartans: Bella Reay
Spartans: L James, H Malone, N Fairless, A Sample, M O'Brien, B Metcalf (capt.), A Read, L Lowry, B Reay, A N Other, J Morgan
Slipway: M Horne, G Chambers, M Short, M Hayton, M Mulligan, B Turnbull (capt.), M Quinn, M Gray, V Bryant, A McConnell, L McConnell.

1917-11-03 *Armstrong's Naval Yard 4 - Angus Sanderson's Munitionettes 0*
Munitionettes' Cup R1, played at the Hollymount ground, Bedlington, raising £120 in aid of the Tyneside Scottish Committee.
Scorers: Scott, Heron, Jane, Ruddock.

1917-11-03 *Rise Carr 3 - Darlington Railway Athletic 1*
Munitionettes' Cup R1
Scorer: Hooper (3) for Rise Carr.
Rise Carr: L. Johnson, A. Park, G. Ashton, L. Roberts, J. Lodge, M. Apperton, F. Atkinson, Mrs Lythe, S. Hooper, S. Scullion, H. Blewett
Railway Athletic: Brown, Martin, Greenhalgh, Atkinson, Bush, Haddikan, Pearson, Pockett, Worster, McCleod, McCleod.

1917-11-03 *Workington 3 - Carlisle 0*
Played at Lonsdale Park in aid of the Red Cross Xmas Gifts Fund
Scorer: S. Watchorn (2), E. McKay.

1917-11-10 *Palmer's 2 - Birtley Cartridge Case Factory 2*
Munition Girls' Cup R1 (replay) played at Chester-le-Street in aid of the Chester-le-Street Soldiers' Christmas Parcels Fund.
Scorers: M. Dodd, L. Young for Palmer's; S Matthews (2 - 1 pen) for Birtley.
The Palmer's team left the field after disputing a penalty three minutes before full time, and an emergency meeting of the Cup Committee on 13th November awarded the tie to Birtley.

1917-11-10 *Wallsend Slipway Munitionettes 0 - Wallsend North-East Munitionettes 0*
Played at Willington in aid of Willington Distinguished Heroes' Fund and Brancepeth Castle V.A.D. Hospital for Wounded Soldiers.

1917-11-10 *Brown's 1 - Slipway United 0*
Played at West Hartlepool in aid of the local Federation of Discharged Soldiers and Sailors.
Scorer: N. Kirk
(Note: this probably refers to Shipyard United).

1917-11-17 *Blyth Spartans Ladies 4 - Gosforth Aviation Athletic Ladies 2*
Munition Girls' Cup R1, played at New Delaval in aid of the St John's Ambulance Brigade.
Scorers: B Reay (2), Dolly Allen, A. Read for Spartans; E. Waters (2) for Gosforth.
Spartans: L James, H Malone, N Fairless, A Sample, M O'Brien, B Metcalf (capt.), A Read, L Lowery, B Reay, D Allen, J Morgan
Gosforth (from): J Steel, F Tweddle, J Sims, E Johnson, M Best, E Waters, E Young, E Irwin, E Spedding, D Connolly, M Leach, M Carr, S Mansfield.

1917-11-17 *Glaholm & Robson 4 - Hood Haggie's Willington 0*
Played at Sunderland Rovers ground, Hendon (half-time score); the match raised more than £80 for the Red Cross Society
Glaholm & Robson (blue): M Scott, S Armstrong, S Whiteside, A Thwaites, G Wooton, F Day, Buckley, S Fox, J Wright, G Lincoln, Pattison; reserves: A Young, C Mordey
Haggies (red): E Greig, C Robson, F Deardon, A Fannon, E Tuch, R Rix, E Saunders, M Blake, J Duff, M Rowans, A Mallon.

1917-11-17 *Sacriston Munition Ladies 2 - No 60 Shop Scotswood Ladies 1*
Played at Sacriston in aid of the local bed in the St. John Ambulance Hospital in France.
Scorers: I Willis for Scotswood; S Matthews (2 - 1 pen) for Sacriston.

1917-11-17 *Expansion 2 - Darlington Munitionettes 0*
Played at Feethams, Darlington, in aid of the Soldiers' and Sailors' Comforts Fund.
Scorers: Jessie Spenceley, H. Agar.

1917-11-17 *Angus Sanderson's Girls 1 - 40 Shop Girls 0*

1917-11-24 *Dorman Long 1 - Richardson, Westgarth's 1*
Munition Girls' Cup R1 played at the Victoria Ground, Stockton before 2,000 spectators in aid of the Sailors' and Minesweepers' Orphans Fund.
Scorers: McGuire for Dorman's; O'Neil for Richardson's.

1917-11-24 *Samuelson's 3 - Richardson, Westgarth's 3*
Reported as Munition Girls' Cup R2, but does not tie in with other results. It may refer to Darlington Rise Carr v Richardson Westgarth's No. 2 played at Samuelson's ground.

1917-11-24 *Bolckow, Vaughan 4 - Ridley's (Skinningrove) 1*
Munition Girls' Cup R2.

1917-11-24 *Armstrong Whitworth 43 Shop 1 - Armstrong Whitworth 57 Shop 1*
Played at Mickley, to "reduce the deficit on the recent children's' gala."

1917-11-24 *Armstrong Whitworth 43 Shop 4 - Wounded Warriors 6*
Played at Stanley in aid of the NW Durham Branch of the Discharged and Demobilised Sailors' and Soldiers' Federation. The Wounded Warriors comprised 8 one-legged men and two one-armed men from the Cowen Rehabilitation Home at Benwell.
Scorers: H March (4) for 43 Shop; Clarkson (3 - 2 pen), Harvey and Farnish for the Wounded Warriors.

1917-11-24 *Websters Munitionettes 1 - Glaholm & Robson Munitionettes 1*
Played at High Barnes.

1917-12-01 *Armstrong-Whitworth 2 - Vickers 1*
Played at St James's Park before 14,000 spectators for the benefit of munitionettes employed at Armstrong-Whitworth's
Scorers: Sarah Cornforth (pen), Bella Willis
Armstrong's: A. Shaw (60 Shop), G. Battista (60 Shop), J. Turnbull (Birtley CCF), R. Cole (60 Shop), B. Will's (60 Shop), N. Innes (58 Shop), I. Spedding (Aviation), E. Fairbairn (57 Shop), S. Cornforth (Birtley CCF), E. Wallace (57 Shop), H. Ruddock (Naval Yard).

1917-12-01 *Dorman Long (No. 1) 0 - Richardson, Westgarth's (No. 1) 0*
Munition Girls' Cup R1 replay, played at Samuelson's Athletic ground, Middlesbrough, in aid of Jack's Bairns Day and Munition Workers Relations' (Soldiers and Sailors) Christmas Parcels Fund.
Westgarth's: Hawthorne, Quigley, Barnett, Bailey, Clarke, Downing, Dunning, Jefferson, Sidebottom, Robinson, O'Neill
Dorman's: Hodge, Price, Dulsee, Williams, McQuade, Ward, Simmons, Robinson, McGuire, Humphrey, McMasters.

1917-12-01 *Brown's 1 - Expansion 0*
Played at West Hartlepool in aid of the Durham Light Infantry Prisoners of War Fund.

1917-12-01 *Blyth Spartans 5 - Sunderland Ladies 0*

Played at Hendon in aid of the Sunderland Discharged Soldiers' and Sailors' Federation. (Spartans were named in the Sunderland Echo as 'Blyth Spurs')

Spartans: L James, H Malone, N Fairless, A Sample, N O'Brien, B Metcalfe (capt.), A Reed, A Allen, B Reay, D Allen, J Morgan; Reserve: D Summers.

1917-12-08 *Richardson Westgarth (No 2) 0 - Darlington Rise Carr 0*

Munitionettes' Cup R3, played at Ayresome Park in aid of the Northern Echo Soldiers' and Sailors' Comforts Fund.

1917-12-08 *Palmers' Munitionettes 3 - Foster, Blackett & Wilson's Munitionettes 1*

Played at Hebburn Black Watch ground.

Palmers: S Scott, L Weightman, L Gibson, M Bainbridge, L Form, A Fawcus, E Graham, M Todd, C Connan, L Young, L McCauley.

1917-12-08 *40 Shop Newcastle 1 - 58 Shop Scotswood 1*

Played at Annfield Plain in aid of St John's Ambulance and the British Red Cross.

Scorers: J. Mills for 40 Shop and S Henderson for 58 Shop.

1917-12-08 *Wallsend Slipway 0 - NE Marine 0*

Played at Wallsend in aid of the Mayor of Wallsend's War Fund.

1917-12-08 *Gosforth Aviation 3 - Hood Haggies 0*

1917-12-08 *Browns v Central Marine*

Played at Thornley in aid of the Thornley Disabled Soldiers' and Sailors' Fund.

1917-12-08 *Websters's 1 - Sunderland Ladies 0*

1917-12-08 *Dorman's (No. 1) v R.A.M.C. Stockton*

Women v Men match played at the Victoria ground, Stockton in aid of the Beechgrove Military Hospital. The men played with hands tied behind their backs.

1917-12-15 *Blyth Spartans Ladies 5 - Newcastle Ladies 0*

Played at Morpeth Road, Blyth in aid of the "Our Day" effort of the Red Cross. The Newcastle Ladies were actually the team from Angus Sanderson's works.

Scorers: B. Reay (4 – 1 pen), D. Allen

Spartans: L James, M Malone, N Fairless, A Sample, M O'Brien, B Metcalfe (capt.), A Reed, N Allen, B Reay, D Allen, J Morgan, reserve: D Gammers

Newcastle: M Lowery, B Smith, M Miller, E Henderson, M Charlton, L Dixon, L Bell, K Phillips, L E Lowes (capt.), L Gransbury, E Ormston, reserve: L Carr.

1917-12-15 *South Bank Ladies 3 - Middlesbrough Ladies 2*

Trial match played at Normanby Road, South Bank, to select a team to represent Teesside against Tyneside. Proceeds in aid of the "Northern Echo" Soldiers' and Sailors' Comforts Fund.

South Bank: E. Wells (Smith's Dock), R. Wells (Smith's Dock), V. Martin (Bolckow's), A. Farrell, E. Milner (Bolckow's), C. Conway, S. English, L. Edwards (Smith's Dock), W. McKenna, A. Wharton, A. Leach (Bolckow's); reserves: M. Wyley (Smith's Dock), A. Hartley (Smith's Dock), G. Rees (Bolckow's)

Middlesbrough: A. Briggs (Clarence), B. Quigley, M. Barnett (Westgarth's), F. Agar (Dorman's No. 2), R. Boyle, L. Lawrence (Clarence), L. Dunn (Dorman's No. 2), G. Jefferson (Westgarth's), M. Vinckley (Dorman's No. 2), A. McIntyre (Clarence); reserves: G. Hawthorne (Westgarth's), J. Clay (Clarence).

1917-12-15 *Probables 1 - Possibles 1*

Trial match played at Wallsend to pick a team to represent the North-East in a match versus the North of Ireland Munition Girls, to be played at Belfast on Boxing Day.

Scorers: Turnbull, Bryant.

Probables: Horn (Slipway), Weygood (North-Eastern), Short (Slipway), Mulligan (Slipway), Carrot (North-Eastern), Hayton (Willington Foundry), Dorrian (West Hartlepool), Kirk (West Hartlepool), Jackson (North Eastern), Bryant (Slipway), McConnell (Slipway).

Possibles: Scott (Jarrow), Sepine (Sunderland), Chambers (Slipway), Catterick (North-Eastern), Reay (Blyth), Turnbull (Slipway), Watson (Hood Haggie), Grey (Slipway), Cornforth (Birtley), Connell (Swan and Hunter), Scott (North-Eastern).

1917-12-15 *Brown's 4 - Belle Vue 1*
Played at Easington in aid of the village Wounded Soldiers Welcome Home Fund
Scorers: N. Murray (3), E. Ferguson for Browns; T Sherry for Belle Vue.

1917-12-21 *Foster Blackett & Wilson's Ladies 1 - Palmers Girls 3*
Played at Hebburn Black Watch ground.

1917-12-22 *Wearside Girls 2 - Teesside Girls 4*
Played at Sunderland Rovers ground, Hendon, in aid of the widow of the late Mr. Shepherd.
Scorers: McKenna (2), Leech and Jefferson for Teesside; Lawson and Whiteside for Wearside.
Teesside: A Briggs (Dorman's, Clarence), B. Quigley (Richardson Westgarth's No. 1), A. Dukes (Dorman's No. 1), A. Farrell (Bolckow's), R. Boyle (Dorman's Clarence), L. Robson (Dorman's Clarence), S. English (Smith's Dock), G. Jefferson (Richardson Westgarth's No. 1), W. McKenna (capt., Bolckow's), M. McKinstry (Dorman's No. 2), A. Leach (Bolckow's); Reserves: J. Hodge (Dorman's No. 1), R. Wells (Smith's Dock), J. Adams (Dorman's No. 2)
Wearside: Scott (Glaholm & Robson), N English (Sunderland Ladies), Alice Kidney (Webster's), S. McCormack (Sunderland Ladies), G Hooton (Glaholm & Robson), B Halliday (Webster's), M McCulley (Webster's), Amy Smith (Sunderland Ladies), V Lowson (Webster's), G Lincoln and S Patterson (Glaholm & Robson); Reserves: H Nobbe, J Crosby (Sunderland Ladies), E Beatty and E Sanderson (Webster's).

1917-12-25 *Blyth Spartans Ladies 6 - Gosforth Aviation Ladies 0*
Played at Cowpen Square, Blyth, in aid of the Duke of Wellington Christmas Parcels Fund
Scorers; B. Reay (3), D Allen, J. Morgan, A. Sample.

1917-12-26 *Palmer's Munitionettes 3 - Hood Haggie's Munitionettes 0*

Played at Jarrow in aid of a fund to provide gifts to wounded soldiers in the Jarrow and Hebburn VAD Hospital (raised £20)

Scorers: Graham (2 - 1 penalty), Connan

Palmers: Scott, Gibson, Weightman, Young, Form, Bainbridge, Graham, Fawcus, Connan, Todd, McCauley

Hood Haggies: Greig, Dearden, Pix, Fannon, Tuck, Craig, Cook, Williams, Bolland, Storey, Blake.

1917-12-26 *Tyneside Girls 4 - Irish Girls 1*

Played at Grosvenor Park, Belfast, before 20,000 spectators in aid of war charities.

Scorers: Dorrian, Jackson, Cornforth (pen), Kirk for Tyneside, Scott for Belfast

Woman of the match: Bella Carrott.

Tyneside: Margaret Scott (Palmers), Hilda Weygood (NEM), Maggie Short (Wallsend Slipway), Bella Willis (50 Shop), Bella Carrott (capt. NEM), Bella Turnbull (Wallsend Slipway), Mary Dorrian (Brown's), Nellie Kirk, (Brown's), Sarah Cornforth (Birtley), Ethel Jackson (NEM), Lizzie McConnell (Wallsend Slipway).

1917-12-26 *Dorman, Long (No.2) 2 - Smith's Dock 0*

Munitionettes' Cup R2 played at Normanby Road, South Bank. Smith's Dock lodged a protest, and the match was ordered to be replayed on 5th January 1918

Scorers: McKinchley (pen), A. N. Other.

1917-12-26 *Armstrong Whitworth 57 Shop 1 - Armstrong Whitworth 60 Shop 0*

Played at Dene Park, Hexham before 1,000 spectators, raising £34 for the Red Cross Society and the Hexham War Hospital Supply Depot.

Scorer: Miss Andrews. (The winning team fielded only 9 players).

1917-12-26 *Webster's v Glaholm & Robson*

Scheduled for Boxing Day at Sunderland Rovers ground, Hendon, in aid of D.L.I. funds. Postponed to 19-1-1918 due to snow, again postponed to 16-2-1918.

1917-12-29 *Blyth Spartans Munitions Girls 1 - Wallsend Slipway Munitions Girls 0*

Played at Portland Park, Ashington before 2,500 spectators in aid of the Ashington Soldiers and Sailors Xmas Gifts Fund.

Scorer: Bella Reay

Spartans: L. James, H. Malone, N. Fairless, A. Sample, M. O'Brien, B. Metcalfe (capt.), A. Reed, N. Allen, B. Reay, A. Allen, J. Morgan; Reserves: E. Foster, D. Summers

Slipway: M. Horne, G. Chambers, M. Short, M. Hayton, M. Mulligan, B. Turnbull (capt.), M. Quinn, M. Gray, V. Bryant, A. McConnell.

1917-12-29 *Armstrong's Naval Yard v Hood Haggies*

Played at the Parade Ground, Walker, in aid of Private George Brunton, who lost his arm in Armstrong's low yard.

Naval Yard: Heron, Patton, Watson, Jane. Litster, Nendick (capt.), Thomson, Johnson, Gatherer, Kell, Ruddock.

Hood Haggie's: Grey, Rix, Dearden, Craig, Tuck, Fannen, Storey, Blake, Bollend, Williams, Martin.

1917-12-29 *Armstrong-Whitworth 57 Shop 1 - Birtley Cartridge Case Girls 0*

Munitionettes' Cup R2, played at Scotswood.

1918-01-02 *Blyth Spartans Ladies 10 - Sunderland Ladies 0*

Played at Croft Park, Blyth before 5,000 spectators in aid of the Blyth Red Cross War Supply Depot. The Sunderland Ladies were actually the team from Webster's Rope works.

Scorers: Bella Reay (6), N Allen (2), D Allen, A Reed

Spartans: L. James, H. Malone, N. Fairless, A. Sample, M. O'Brien, B. Metcalfe (capt.), A. Reed, N. Allen, B. Reay, D. Allen, J. Morgan; Reserves: E. Forster, D. Summers

Sunderland: W. Moon, C. McNully, B. Kidney, M. Buddington, L. Beattie, B. Halliday, M. Watson, M. McNully, V. Lawson, H. Sanderson, B. Rodgers; Reserves: Hall, Davison, Donkin.

1918-01-02 *Rise Carr v NER Ladies*

1918-01-05 *Wallsend Slipway Munitionettes v North Eastern Marine Munitionettes*

Played at Station Road, Forest Hall, in aid of the Longbenton Sailors' and Soldiers' Pensions Emergency Fund, referee, W McCracken

Wallsend Slipway: M Horne, G Chambers, A Yewman, M Gray, M Short, B Turnbull, A McConnell, M Clarke, M Mulligan, M Thompson, V Bryant
North East Marine: A Nelson, F Rothwell, H Weygood, E Catterick, B Carrott, B Holloran, F Wallace, J McCarron, E Jackson, M Atkins, E Scott.

1918-01-05 *Dorman Long (No 2) 1 - Smiths Dock 0*
Munition Girls' Cup R2.

1918-01-12 *Blyth Spartans Munitionettes 7 - North East Marine Munitionettes 1*
Munition Girls' Cup R2 played at St James's Park in aid of the Cowen Training Home for Disabled Soldiers and Sailors
Scorers: Bella Reay (6), A Reed for Blyth, Wilson for NEM.

1918-01-12 *Vickers (Barrow) 2 - Armstrong-Whitworth (Newcastle) 0*
Played at Holker Street, Barrow.
Scorers: L. Parton, A. Bradley
Vickers: J. Percival, G. Tindall, L. Wagstaff, M. Christian, L. Michaelson, S. McClellan, A. Fletcher, W. Bradley, M. Holmes, L. Parton, M. Dickinson
Armstrong's: A. Shaw, G. Battista, J. Turnbull, B. Cole, B. Willis, N. Innes, L. Spedding, E. Fairbairn, S. Cornforth, E. Wallace, H. Ruddock.

1918-01-12 *Brown's 2 - Railway Athletic 0*
Played at Cornforth United Ground, West Cornforth, in aid of West Cornforth Ladies' Working Party
Scorer: Kirk (2)

1918-02-02 *Armstrong Whitworth 57 Shop 2 - Armstrong Whitworth 60 Shop 1*
Munition Girls' Cup quarter-final played at Scotswood
Scorers: Ethel Wallace, E Cole for 57 Shop, Florrie Taylor for 60 Shop.

1918-02-02 *Teesside Munitionettes 1 - Tyneside Munitionettes 1*
Played at Stockton before 2,000 spectators (postponed from 19th January due to ground conditions)

Scorers: Bella Reay for Tyneside, Winnie McKenna for Teesside
Tyneside: Margaret Scott (Palmers Jarrow), Julia Turnbull (Birtley), Florrie Deardon (Hood Haggies), Isabella Willis (Armstrong's 60 Shop), Isabella Carrot (N.E. Marine)(capt.), Martha Lowthian (Armstrong's 57 Shop), Isabella Thompson (Armstrong's Naval Yard), Ethel Jackson (N.E. Marine), Isabella Reay (Blyth Spartans), Minnie Seed (Gosforth Aerodrome Aviation), Agnes McConnell (Wallsend Slipway); reserves: Elizabeth Form (Palmer's), Hilda Ruddock (Armstrong's Naval Yard)
Teesside: V. Hodge (Dorman's No. 1), A. Farrell (Bolckow's), E. Ashton (Darlington), A. Appleton (Darlington), M. O'Connell (Westgarth's No. 2), A. Wharton (Bolckow's), L. Dunne (Dorman's No. 2), G. Jefferson (Westgarth's No. 1) (capt.), W. McKenna (Bolckow's), M. McKinstry (Dorman's No. 2), A. Leach (Bolckow's); reserves: V. Hawthorne (Westgarth's No. 1), A. O'Neill (Dorman's No. 2), N. Hartley and S. English (Smith's Dock).

1918-02-02 *Newcastle Ladies 2 - Sunderland Ladies 1*
Played at Southwick before 2,000 spectators in aid of the Jeffrey Hospital, Monkwearmouth.
Scorers: Dixon, Lowes for Newcastle; Crosby (pen) for Sunderland.
Newcastle: Donnelly, Smith, Miller, Lowrey, Charlton, Dixon, Ormston, Bell, Lowes, Gransbury, Chillips, (res.) Foster
Sunderland: Dorrian, English, Crosby, McCormick, Walker, Woodie, Noble, Catchesides, Cotherson, Hardy, Young, (res.) Crooks.

1918-02-09 *Blyth Spartans Munitionettes 4 - Palmers Jarrow Munitionettes 2*
Played at Morpeth Road, Blyth in aid of the Blyth Discharged Soldiers' and Sailors' Federation.
Blyth: M. Spinks, H. Malone, N. Fairless, A. Sample, M. O'Brien, B. Metcalf, A. Reed, A. Allan, B. Reay, D. Allan, J. Morgan
Palmers: (from) A. Wylis, M. Scott, K. Weightman, E. Gibson, M. Bainbridge, E. Form, L. Green, M. Donnelly, L. Macaulay, E. Young, E. Graham, M. Todd, C. Coundon, F. Coundon.

1918-02-09 *Armstrong-Whitworth 57 Shop 1 - Armstrong-Whitworth 58 Shop 1*
Played at Bute Park, Dipton, before 1,000 spectators, in aid of deceased Soldier's and Sailors' dependents
Scorers: Fox for 57 Shop, Charlton for 58 Shop.

1918-02-11 *Wallsend Slipway 6 - North East Marine 0*

1918-02-16 *Darlington Rise Carr 2 - Dorman Long (No. 2) 1*
Munitionettes' Cup R3.

1918-02-16 *ABP & Co. 0 - Dorman, Long Port Clarence 1*
Played at Stockton
Scorer: A. White
Ashmore, Benson: F. Dodds, E. Thomas, J. Davis, M. Glancey, J. Templeman, A. Todd, J. Brown, M. Evis, V. Trueman (capt.), K. Ridley, E. Hall
Dorman, Long: A. Brigg (capt), L. Donnelly, M. Robinson, N. Fewster, L. Gallagher, A. McIntyre, A. Lewis, I. Clay, A. Hardiman, A. White.

1918-02-16 *Webster & Co. Ladies 2 - Glaholm & Robson's Ladies 1*
Played at Sunderland Rover's ground, Hendon, before several thousand spectators, in aid of the D.L.I. Prisoners of War Fund.
Scorers: Lawson, Wright (pen) for Glaholm; Sanderson for Websters
Glaholm: M. Adamson, J. Parker, Anderson, A. Thwaites, G. Wooton, F. Day, A. Buckley, C. Mordey, J. Wright, G. Lincoln, J. Patterson
Webster's: C. McCulley, B. Donkin, A. Kidney, M. Buddington, K. Murray, B. Holliday, M. Watson, E. Sanderson, J. Tomlinson, V. Lawson, M. Russell.

1918-02-16 *Browns's (West Hartlepool) 3 - Bolckow, Vaughan & Co. (Middlesbrough) 2*

1918-02-21 *Angus Sanderson 1 - Gosforth Aviation 1*

1918-02-23 *Foster Blackett & Wilson's Girls 1 - Webster's Girls 1*

1918-02-23 *Armstrong College Ladies 7 - Chester-le-Street Ladies 1*

1918-02-23 *Armstrong-Whitworth 57 Shop 1 - Armstrong-Whitworth 60 Shop 1*
Played at Ryton, in aid of the West Ryton and Crawcrook Recognition Fund.

1918-02-23 *Angus Sanderson Girls 1 - Gosforth Aviation Girls 1*

1918-02-23 *Blyth Spartans 3 - Armstrongs Naval Yard 0*
Munitionettes' Cup quarter-final played at Westoe in aid of the Sailors and Minesweepers Orphans' Fund.
Scorers: Reay (2), Allen.

1918-02-23 *Bolckow, Vaughan 2 - Dorman Long No 1 1*
Munitionettes' Cup quarter-final played at Samuelson's Athletic ground, Middlesbrough.
Scorers: McKenna (2 - 1 pen) for Bolckows; Robinson for Dorman Long
Bolckow's were awarded a penalty close on time, which led to a protest after the match. The Cup Committee decided that the referee's decision should stand.

1918-02-23 *ABP & Co. 1 - Westgarth's Middlesbrough 0*
Played at the Rugby field, Stockton
Scorer: Ridley
Ashmores: Bell, Davis, Dodds, A. Todd, Templeman, Glancey, E. Ritchie, E. Ridley, V. Trueman (capt), M. Evis, E. Brown
Westgarth's: G. Drennan, E. Allen, I. Fentiman, L. Bailey, M. O'Connell, A. Denny, G. Goodman, B. Potts, N. Nistram, O. Smith.

1918-02-23 *Sacriston Ladies v Houghton Ladies*
Played at Philadelphia cricket ground, South Sacriston in aid of the Disabled Soldiers' Fund
Sacriston: H. Mordue, M. Storey, F. Lambeth, M. Biddle, E. Thompson, J. Turnbull, N. Clark, S. Ewen, M. Mallabar, E. Moffat, F. Stockdale.

1918-03-02 *Tyneside Munitionettes 3 - Teesside Munitionettes 0*
Played at St James's Park in aid of St Dunstan's Hostel for Blinded Soldiers and Sailors.
Scorers: Wallace (2), Jackson
Tyneside (green and white): E. James (Blyth Spartans), F. Dearden (Hood, Haggie's), E. Short (Wallsend Slipway), E. Form (Palmer's), S. Cornforth (Birtley), M. Lothian (57 Shop), A Reed (Blyth Spartans), E. Jackson (North Eastern Marine), B. Reay (Blyth Spartans), M. Seed (Gosforth Aviation), H Ruddick (Armstrong's Naval Yard)

Teesside (scarlet and white): J. Hodge (Dorman, Long & Co.), A. Farrell (Bolckow, Vaughan & Co.), A. Dukes (Dorman, Long & Co.), M. O'Connell (Richardson, Westgarths & Co.), R. Boyle (Dorman, Long & Co.), J. Lodge (Darlington), N. Humphries (Dorman, Long & Co.), G Jefferson (Richardson, Westgarths & Co.), W. McKenna (Bolckow, Vaughan & Co.), M. McKinstry (Dorman, Long & Co.), A. Leech (Bolckow, Vaughan & Co.)

1918-03-02 *Angus Sanderson Girls 0 - Haggie's Girls 0*

1918-03-02 *ABP & Co. 1 - Smiths Dock 3*

Played at the Old Rugby Field, Stockton.

Scorers: Conway (pen), Edwards for Smiths Dock; Ritchie for Ashmore Benson (Trueman missed a penalty)

Ashmore, Benson: A. Bell, Dods, Davis, N. Coote, Templeman, A. Todd, Ritchie, Ridley, Trueman, Evis, Brown

Westgarths: Green, Well, Wylie, Powell, Well, McNeil, English, Conway, Edwards, Willis, Moody.

1918-03-09 *Blyth Spartans 2 - Armstrong Whitworth (57 Shop) 1*

Munition Girls' Cup semi-final played at St James's Park before 10,000 spectators in aid of the Munitionettes' Parcel Fund and the Armstrong-Whitworth Girls' Benevolent Fund.

Scorers: A. Allen, B. Reay for Spartans; E. Wallace for 57 Shop

1918-03-09 *Westgarths 0 - ABP 1*

Played at Middlesbrough.

1918-03-09 *Bolckow, Vaughan 1 - Darlington Rise Carr 1*

Played at the Forge Albion ground, Darlington in aid of Sailors' and Minesweepers' Orphans.

1918-03-09 *Wallsend Slipway Munitionettes 1 - North East Marine Munitionettes 0*

Played at Rosehill, Wallsend, in aid of the Comfort Fund for Willington Quay Soldiers and Sailors.

Slipway: Watson, Chambers, Short, Hayton, Milligan, Turnbull, A. McConnell, Jackson, Cornforth, Bryant, L McConnell.

1918-03-09 *unnamed teams*

Played at Throckley in aid of the Throckley Heroes' Presentation Fund.

1918-03-16 *Bolckow, Vaughan 1 - Darlington Rise Carr 0*
Munition Girls' Cup semi-final replay played at South Bank.
Scorer: Winnie McKenna.

1918-03-16 *Dorman, Long Combined XI 1 - Rest of the League 1*
Played at the Victoria Ground, Hartlepool before 500 spectators.
Scorers: Dukes for Dorman's, Ridley for The Rest.

1918-03-16 *Birtley 4 - Gosforth Aviation 0*
Played at Pelton Fell in aid of the local Soldiers' and Sailors' Fund. Gosforth had only 8 players, and borrowed 2 from Birtley to make a 10-a-side game.

1918-03-18 *Hood Haggie's Munitionettes 0 - Internationals 4*
Played at the Old Cycling Enclosure, Wallsend, in aid of the Comrades of the Great War Association.
Scorers: Cornforth (3), Jackson.
Internationals: Horne* (Wallsend Slipway), Weygood (N. E. Marine), Short (Wallsend Slipway), Catterick* (Birtley), Carrott (N. E. Marine), Turnbull (Wallsend Slipway), S. Henderson* (No. 58 Shop, Elswick), Jackson (N. E. Marine), Cornforth (Birtley), Bryant* and L. McConnell (Wallsend Slipway); *Reserves:* Mulligan (Wallsend Slipway), M. Carron (N. E. Marine).
* Substitutes for internationals unable to play on this occasion.

1918-03-23 *Blyth Spartans 4 - Armstrong-Whitworth 60 Shop 1*
Played at Bebside in aid of the Bebside Military Merit Fund
Scorers: Reay (3) A. N. Other for Spartans; Willis for 60 Shop.

1918-03-23 *Browns 2 - Darlington Rise Carr 0*
Played at the Victoria Ground, Hartlepool, in aid of the Missions to Seamen
Scorer: Kirk (2 – 1 pen).

1918-03-29 *Durham 4 - Northumberland 1*
Played at St James's Park before 5,000 spectators in aid of the Cowen Home for the Training of Disabled Soldiers and Sailors.
Scorers: Wallace for Northumberland; Cornforth (4 - 1 pen) for Durham.

Durham: M. Scott (Foster, Blackett & Wilson and Jarrow), I. Smith (Angus Sanderson and Jarrow), J. Turnbull (Birtley CC), E. Form (Palmer's Jarrow), B. Carrott (North Eastern Marine and Gateshead), J. Miller (58 Shop Scotswood and Gateshead), M. Dorrian, N. Kirk (Brown's Girls, West Hartlepool), S. Cornforth (Birtley and Pelton), M. Seed (Gosforth Aviation and Sunderland), H. Ruddock (Naval Yard and Ryhope); reserves: A. Shaw (60 Shop), E. E. Lowes (Angus-Sanderson)

Northumberland: N. Heron (Naval Yard), F. Dearden (Hood, Haggie's, Willington), M. Short (Wallsend Slipway), B. Willis (60 Shop and Prudhoe), E. Andrews (57 Shop and Newcastle), B. Wallace (Wallsend Slipway), E. Fairbairn (57 Shop and North Shields), E. Wallace (57 Shop and Newcastle), S. Henderson (58 Shop and Newcastle), E. Jackson (Wallsend North Eastern Marine), E McConnell (Wallsend Slipway); reserves: E. Cole (North Shields and 57 Shop), G. Battista (Newcastle and 60 Shop), M. Nendick (Walker Naval Yard), A. Spedding (Aviation, Newcastle).

1918-03-30 *Bolckow, Vaughan 0 - Blyth Spartans 0*

Munitionettes' Cup Final played at St James's Park.

Spartans: L. James, H. Malone, N. Fairless, A. Sample, M. O'Brien, B. Metcalfe (capt.), A. Reed, A. Allen, B. Reay, D. Allen, J. Morgan.

1918-03-30 *Browns 0 - Expansion 0*

Played at the Caledonian Ground before 500 spectators in aid of "Eggs for Wounded Soldiers" (the following day was Easter Sunday).

1918-03-30 *Glaholm & Robson Ltd. 1 - Armstrong Whitworth No. 58 Shop 1*

Played at Ashbrooke in aid of the Sunderland Royal Infirmary Ladies' Guild

Glaholm: M. Anderson, S. Parker, S. Whiteside, A. Thwaites, G. Wooton, F. Day, A. Buckley, C. Mordey, J. Wright, G. Lincoln, J. Patterson; reserves S. Fox, C. Dodds

58 Shop: T. Jennings, A. Armstrong, M. Henderson, N. Charlton, C. Short, R. Drinkald, M. Glass, A. Charlton, S. Henderson, M. Jameson, J. Leighton; reserves: A. Watson, F. Gallagher.

1918-03-30 *unnamed teams*
Played at Cornmoor Road, Whickham, in aid of the Whickham War Memorial and Recognition Fund. Bill McCracken to referee.

1918-04-01 *Blyth Spartans 4 - Palmer's Ladies 2*
Played at Jarrow
Scorers: A. Reed, B. Reay, V. Bryant (2) for Spartans.

1918-04-01 *Foster Blackett & Wilson's Munitionettes 1 - Walker Naval Yard 0*

1918-04-01 *Browns 2 - Dorman, Long & Co. 0*
Played at the Victoria Ground, Hartlepool before 500 spectators in aid of the "Indigent Sick"
Scorer: Murray (2)
(this was the half-time score).

1918-04-01 *Angus Sanderson 6 - Horner's Dainty Dinahs 0*
Played at the University Ground, Durham in aid of Comrades of the Great War, raising £51 2s 2d.
(This was the Dainty Dinahs' first game – after just 1 week's practice).

1918-04-01 *Angus Sanderson 0 - Birtley 0*
Played at the University Ground, Durham
Birtley had been due to play Darlington, who did not arrive, so Sandersons played a second game.
Both games raised a total of £51 2s 2_d for Comrades of the Great War.

1918-04-02 *Houghton Munition Workers (Ladies) 1 - Glaholm Robson & Co. 0*

1918-04-04 *Blyth Shipyard Munitions Ladies 7 - Anti-Aircraft Section 1*
Women versus Men match; Blyth Shipyard Ladies was a newly-formed team.

1918-04-05 *Webster's Ladies v Hebburn Ladies (Lead Works)*
To be played at Ashbrooke in aid of the Royal Institute for the Blind; the Hebburn Lead Works was Foster, Blackett & Wilson.

1918-04-06 *Glaholm Robson's 2 - Hood Haggie's Munitionettes 2*
Played at the Wallsend Slipway ground in aid of the Mayor of Wallsend's Relief Fund.
Haggies: R. Rix, F. Dearden, E. Tuck, A. Fannen, M. A. Gatherer, A. Craig, E. Cooke, S. Clark, E. Robson, M. Blake, L. Williams; Reserve: C. Robertson.

1918-04-17 *Palmers Munitionettes 4 - Navy Theatricals 1*
Women v Men match (both in fancy dress) played at the Hebburn Shipyard Recreation Ground in aid of the Hebburn Ladies' Sewing Party
Scorers: Mary Lyons (2), Lizzie Green, Lizzie Gibson for the ladies; "Charlie Chaplin" for the sailors.

1918-04-20 *Carlisle Munition Girls 0 - Blyth Spartans 3*
Played at Brunton Park, Carlisle, in aid of the Carlisle Citizens' League for the Borderers Prisoners of War Fund.
Scorers: Allen, Reay (2)
Carlisle: L. Skinner, Mrs Traill (capt.), P. Broadhouse, M. McAdo, E. Bainbridge, V. Newton, S. White, F. Peel, E. Williamson, E. Sowerby, C. Howson
Spartans: L. James, H. Malone, N. Fairless, A. Sample, M. O'Brien, B. Metcalf (capt.), E.. Jackson, A. Allen, B. Reay, M. Lyons, J. Morgan.

1918-04-20 *Sunderland Ladies 0 - Browns 1*
played at Hollow Drift in aid of Minesweepers Widows and Orphans of the German Ocean
Scorer: Mary Dorrian.

1918-04-20 *Birtley C. C. Girls 1 - Elswick Works 58 Shop Girls 0*
Played at Pelton Fell football ground before 500-600 spectators in aid of the Ladies Sewing Party for Soldiers' and Sailors' Comforts.
Scorer: Sally Cornforth
Birtley: Malabar, Middleton, Turnbull, Lishmour, Finlay, Kennedy, Cornforth, Wardle, McKarman, Churcher, Price
Elswick: Jennings, Henderson, Armstrong, Short, Charlton, Drinkald, S. Henderson, Glass, Leightley, H. Charlton, Fitzgerald.

1918-04-20 *Wallsend Slipway v North East Marine*
Played at Blaydon St. Joseph's in aid of the local Heroes' Fund.

1918-04-27 *Blyth Spartans Ladies 0 - Birtley Ladies 0.*
Played at Seaton Delaval in aid of the R.A.O.B. War Annuity Fund. (The match was originally scheduled for 4th April but Birtley took the wrong train and did not arrive till 17:30)
Spartans: L. James, H. Malone, N. Fairless, A. Sample, M. O'Brien, B. Metcalf (capt.), A. Reed, A. Allen, B. Reay, J. Morgan, A. N. Other
Birtley: M. Malabar, N. Middleton, J. Turnbull, M. Kennedy, S. Irwin, M. Finley, M. Little, A. Churches, S. Cornforth, N. Clarke, A. Price.

1918-04-27 *Palmers Munitionettes v Glaholm and Robson's Ladies*

Played at Curlew Road, Jarrow, in aid of "one of Palmer's old players who has been off work for a considerable time owing to illness"

Palmer's (from): S. Scott, A. Malone, K. Weightman, L. Gibson, L. Young, L. Form, L. Green, B. Taylor, E. Graham, M. Lyons, M. Todd, C. Connon, L. McCauley, S. Connon.

1918-04-27 *Wallsend Slipway 2 - Hood Haggie's Girls 0*

Played at Benton Square Mission Ground in aid of the Longbenton War Pensions Fund.

1918-04-27 *Angus Sanderson 2 - Hood Haggie's (South Shore) 0*

Played at Dunston in aid of the War Widows' Relief and Welcome Home Funds.

1918-05-04 *Teesside Munitionettes 4 - Wearside Munitionettes 0*

Played at Normanby Road, South Bank.

Scorers: Jefferson, Dunne, McKenna (2)

Wearside: M. Jane (Armstrong's Naval Yard), N. English (Sunderland), A. Kidney (Webster's), E. Form (Palmer's), E. Lister (Naval Yard), B. Halliday (Webster's), H. Nobble (Sunderland), E. Wallace (Armstrong-Whitworth), V. Lowson (Webster's), M. Seed (Gosforth Aviation), H. Ruddock (Naval Yard);

Teesside: J. Hawthorn (Richardson Westgarth No. 1), A. Farrell (Bolckow, Vaughan), E. Ashton (Darlington), A. Hartley (Smith's Dock), J. Lodge (Darlington), L. Dunne, M. McKinstry (both Dorman, Long No. 2), W. McKenna (Bolckow, Vaughan), G. Jefferson (Richardson Westgarth No. 1), A Dukes (Dorman, Long No. 1).

1918-05-04 *Blyth Spartans 6 - 57 Shop 0*

Played at Croft Park, Blyth (57 Shop had only 9 players)

Scorers: Reay (3) Lyons, Morgan, Allen

Spartans: L. James, Rhodes, Fairless, Sample, O'Brien, Metcalf, Read, Allen Reay, Lyons, Morgan

57 Shop: B. Cole, L. Gould, E. Cole, B. Andrews, A. Hipkin, B. Cappelman, E. Wallace, A. Watson, K. Carr.

1918-05-06 *43 Shop 6 - Grand Fleet selected XI 4*
Women v Men match played at Blaydon Road, Scotswood, in aid of the Scotswood Soldiers' and Sailors' Welcome Home Fund
Scorers: Evans (3), Rooney, Ross, Seaman Quinn (o.g.).

1918-05-11 *Blyth Spartans Munition Ladies 4 - Armstrong Whitworth 60 Shop 2*
Played at St James's Park, Alnwick in aid of the Alnwick branch of the National Federation of Discharged and Demobilised Soldiers and Sailors.
Scorers: Reay (2), Best (2)
Spartans: (from) L. James, R Rhodes, H. Malone, N. Fairless, A. Sample, M. O'Brien, B. Metcalfe, A. Reed, A. Allen, B. Reay, M. Seed, J. Morgan
60 Shop: A. Shaw, G. Battista, C. Irvine, G. Hendry, A. Bowie, E. Gardner, G. Jones, L. Gallagher, B. Willis, N. Neison, F. Taylor.

1918-05-11 *Wallsend Slipway 1 - 58 Shop 0*

1918-05-11 *Palmer's Munitionettes v Angus Sanderson's Munitionettes*
Played at Hebburn Colliery in aid of the Hebburn detachment of the Durham County Volunteer regiment.
Palmer's (from): S. Scott, A. Henderson, K. Weightman, L. Gibson, L. Young, L. Form, L. Green, B. Taylor, E. Graham, M. Lyons, M. Todd, C. Connon, L. McCauley.

1918-05-18 *Bolckow, Vaughan 0 - Blyth Spartans 5*
Munitionettes' Cup Final (replay) played at Ayresome Park, Middlesbrough, in aid of Teesside Medical Charities
Scorers: Reay (3), Lyons, Morgan
Spartans: L. James, H. Weir, N. Fairless, A. Sample, M. O'Brien, B. Metcalfe (capt.), A. Reed, A. Allen, B. Reay, M. Lyons, J. Morgan
Bolckow, Vaughan: G. Kirk, V. Martin, A. Farrell, A. Rowell, E. Milner, A. Wharton, N. Mahon, N. Page, W. McKenna, G. Reece, A. Leach
The final (including the drawn first game) raised £671 10s 5d.

1918-05-18 *Foster Blackett & Wilson's Ladies 1 - North East Marine Ladies 0*
Played at St James's Park in aid of Newcastle Eye Infirmary.

1918-05-18 *Birtley Cartridge Case Shop 3 - Horner's Dainty Dinahs 1*
Played at Chester-le-Street cricket ground in aid of the local Welcome Home Fund. The match was halted for a while in the first half when the ball burst.
Scorers: Cornforth, o.g. (2)
Birtley: Malabar, Middleton, Turnbull, B McManas, Irwin, Finley, Liddle, Churcher, Cornforth (capt.), Clark, Price
Dainty Dinahs: Clifford, Gillespie, Taylor, Hutton, Hunter, Wilson, Watson, Bell, Collingwood, Carr, Kennedy.

1918-05-20 *Angus Sandersons 3 - Craven & Speedy Ropery 0*
played at Hollow Drift in aid of Durham City Branch of Comrades of the Great war; takings £20
Scorer: B Lowes (3).

1918-05-20 *Blyth Spartans 4 - Armstrong Whitworth 58 Shop 0*
Played at Croft Park, Blyth, with the Alfred Wood trophy on display.
Scorers: Reay, Lyons (3).

1918-05-25 *Houghton Ladies 2 - Sunderland Ladies 2*
Played at Murton in aid of the Aged Miners' Homes

1918-05-25 *Browns 0 - Websters 0*
Played at Seaham.

1918-05-26 *Browns 4 - Armstrong-Whitworth 0*
Played at Ferryhill
Scorers: Nellie Kirk (2), Norah Murray (2).

1918-06-01 *Palmers Munition Girls 4 - Walker Naval Yard Munition Girls 0*
Played at Washington in aid of the local branch of Comrades of the Great War.

1918-06-01 *Tyneside Internationals 2 - North of England 2*
Played at St James's Park in aid of the Newcastle branch of Comrades of the Great War; over £100 was taken at the turnstiles.
Scorers: McKenna (2) for the North of England, Cornforth (pen) and Shaw (o.g.) for the Internationals
Tyneside: Maggie Scott (Foster Blacketts, Jarrow), Hilda Weygood (N.E.M.), Maggie Short (Wallsend Slipway), Bella Willis (60 Shop, Scotswood), Bella Carrott capt. (N.E.M.), Violet Bryant (Wallsend Slipway), Mary Dorrian, Nellie Kirk (Brown's, West Hartlepool), Sarah Cornforth (Birtley), Ethel Jackson (N.E.M.), Lizzie McConnell (Wallsend Slipway)

North of England: Ada Shaw (60 Shop & Rowlands Gill), Laura Gould (57 Shop & Scotswood), Amelia Farrell (Bolckows, South Bank), Nellie Stott (Browns, West Hartlepool), Bella Plummer (Expansion, West Hartlepool), Jessie Lodge (Darlington), Lilian Dunne (Middlesbrough), Ethel Wallace (57 Shop & Newcastle), Winnie McKenna (Bolckows, South Bank), Minnie Seed (Sunderland & Aviation), Hilda Ruddock (Naval Yard & Ryhope).

1918-06-01 *Houghton Ladies 5 - Dainty Dinahs 0*
Played at the Lakes Ground, Houghton in aid of the Soldiers' and Sailors' Funds.

1918-06-01 *Blyth Spartans 5 - Carlisle Girls 0*
Played at Croft Park, Blyth, in aid of the Blyth War Widows and Orphans Fund; £31 was taken at the gate. (Reay's hat-trick took her goals total to 113)
Scorers: Reay (3), Allen, O'Brien
Spartans: L. James, H. Weir, N. Fairless, A. Sample, M. O'Brien, B. Metcalfe (capt.), A. Read, A. Allen, B. Reay, S. Rhodes, J. Morgan
Carlisle: L. Skinner, Mrs Traill (capt.), P. Boardhead, M. McAdo, E. Bainbridge, V. Newton, S. White, F. Peel, E. Williamson, E. Lowry, C. Howson.

1918-06-08 *Walker Naval Yard 3 - Foster, Blackett and Wilson's 2*
Played at Park Villa ground, Wallsend, in aid of the St. Dunstan's Hospital for Blinded Soldiers and Sailors.

1918-06-08 *Lady Munition Workers 5 - Ryhope Villa 4*
Women versus Men match played at Ryhope in aid of Comrades of the Great War.

1918-06-15 *Tyneside Munitionettes 0 - Teesside Munitionettes 0*
Played at St James's Park in aid of the Northumberland Prisoners of War Fund.
Tyneside: Ada Shaw (A-W 60 Shop), Grace Battista (A-W 60 Shop), Lizzie March (Brown's 43 Shop), Mary Curry (Foggins 43 Shop), Ettie Andrews (57 Shop), Lizzie Finlay (Birtley), Ada Spedding (Gosforth), Bessie Cole (57 Shop), Ethel Wallace (57 Shop), Sarah Irwin (Birtley), Frances Lister (Foggins 43 Shop)
Teesside: Jennie Hodge (Middlesbrough), Amelia Farrell (South Bank), Emily Ashton, Mary Appleton, Jessie Lodge (all Darlington), Annie Wharton (Everton), Gertie Jefferson (Middlesbrough), Winnie McKenna (South Bank), Maggie McQuire (Middlesbrough), Sarah English (South Bank).

1918-06-15 *Wallsend Slipway Munitionettes 0 - Palmer's Munitionettes 1*
Played at St. Joseph's, Blaydon, in aid of the "Blaydon's Own" Fund.

1918-06-15 *Blyth Spartans 3 - Walker Naval Yard 0*
Played at Croft Park, Blyth
Scorer: Bella Reay (3)
Spartans: (from) L. James, H. Weir, S. Rhodes, N. Fairless, A. Sample, M. O'Brien, B. Metcalfe, A. Reed, A. Allen, B. Reay, M. Lyons, J. Morgan
Naval Yard: N. Heron, L. Litster, M. Watson, M. Meadows, M. Jane, L. Nendick, A. Hill, N. Johnson, M. Seed, E. Scott, H. Ruddock.

1918-06-22 *Hartlepool Munition Girls 0 - Blyth Spartans 1*
Played at the Friarage Field in aid of the Sailors Orphans Fund. Hartlepool were disappointed as only 4 of the Spartans were from Blyth, the rest were from Slipway, NEM and Bolckow's.
Scorer: Bella Reay.

1918-06-22 *Foster, Blackett & Co. 0 - Webster's Girls 0*
Played at Sunderland in aid of Comrades of the Great War.

1918-06-29 *Blyth Spartans Ladies 2 - North of England Munitionettes 0*
Played at Croft Park, Blyth. This match marked the end of Spartan's season, in which they had been undefeated.
Scorer: Bella Reay (2)
Spartans: L. James, S. Rhodes, N. Fairless, A. Sample, M. O'Brien, B. Metcalf, A. Reed, A. Allen, B. Reay, M. Lyons, J. Morgan
North of England: A. Shaw (60 Shop), M. Short (Slipway), A. Farrell (South Bank), B. Willis (60 Shop), E. Jackson (NEM), A. Wharton (South Bank), E. Wallace (57 Shop), M. Seed (Naval Yard), W. McKenna (South Bank), V. Bryant, J. McConnell (Slipway).

1918-06-30 *Palmers Girls 4 - Foster Blackett & Wilson 0*

1918-07-06 *Internationals 1 - North of England Munitionettes 1*
Played at St James's Park before 4,000 spectators in aid of the Y.W.C.A., Huts, Comforts and Munitionettes' Funds. (A re-match of the game played on 1st June)
Scorers: Nellie Stott, Alice Churcher (who must have replaced one of the named players)

Woman of the match: Mary Lyons.

Internationals: Maggie Scott (Foster, Blackett & Wilson, Hebburn), Hilda Weygood (Wallsend N.E.M.), Ethel Jackson (Wallsend Slipway), Bella Willis (60 Shop, Scotswood), Bella Carrot (Wallsend N.E.M., Gateshead), Bella Turnbull (Wallsend Slipway), Mary Dorrian, Nellie Kirk (West Hartlepool), Sarah Cornforth (Birtley), Violet Bryant, Lizzie McConnell (Wallsend Slipway)

North of England: Ada Shaw (60 Shop and Rowlands Gill), Grace Battista (60 Shop, Scotswood), Emily Aston (Darlington), Nellie Stott (West Hartlepool), Jessie Lodge (Darlington), Annie Wharton (South Bank), Minnie Seed (Armstrong's Naval Yard and Sunderland), Winnie McKenna (South Bank), Bella Reay (Blyth Spartans), Mary Lyons (Palmer's, Jarrow), Ethel Wallace (57 Shop, Scotswood).

1918-07-13 *Internationals v Teesside Munitionettes*

Scheduled to be played at Darlington – not reported

1918-07-13 *Houghton-le-Spring Ladies 0 - Horner's Dainty Dinahs 0*

Played at Chester Moor on the occasion of the local Sports Day in aid of the Chester Moor Heroes' Fund.

1918-07-13 *Birtley Munition Girls 5 - Angus Sanderson Newcastle 3*

Played at Usworth in aid of the Aged Miners' Homes.

1918-07-20 *North of England 3 - West of Scotland 2*

Played at St James's Park before 4,000 spectators in aid of the St. Dunstan's Hospital for Blinded Soldiers and Sailors.

Scorers: Winnie McKenna, Sarah Cornforth & Mary Lyons for England; Agnes Connell and Maggie Devlin for Scotland.

North of England: Jennie Hodge (Dorman's, Middlesbrough), Hilda Weygood (Wallsend N.E.M.), Nellie Fairless (Blyth Spartans), Bella Willis (60 Shop Scotswood. and Prudhoe), Sarah Cornforth (Birtley and Pelton), Minnie Seed (Armstrong's Naval Yard, late Gosforth Aviation and Sunderland), Mary Dorrian (Brown's, West Hartlepool), Winnie McKenna (Bolckow's, South Bank, capt.), Bella Reay (Blyth Spartans), Mary Lyons (Palmer's Jarrow), Lizzie McConnell (Wallsend Slipway).

West of Scotland: Jean Brown (Cardonald, Govan), Dolly Cookson (Inchinnan, Paisley, late capt. Vickers FC Barrow), Rosina Clark (Clydesdale), Jean Wilson (Cardonald, Glasgow), Agnes Connell (Mossend, Carfin), Bella Renwick (Mossend, Motherwell), Robina Murdock (Mossend, Motherwell), Nellie McKenzie (Cardonald, Glasgow), Lizzie McWilliams (Clydesdale).

1918-07-27 *Durham v Northumberland*
Played at Bishop Auckland in aid of Jack's Bairns' day.

1918-08-05 *Haggies 0 - Angus Sanderson 3*
Played at the Secondary School, Prince Consort Road, Gateshead in aid of St. Dunstan's Hospital for Blinded Soldiers and Sailors.

1918-08-05 *Palmers Jarrow 2 - Angus Sandersons 0*
Final match in a 5-a-side Munitionettes' Tournament held at St James's Park. Other teams participating: Angus Sandersons, Armstrong's 58 Shop, Armstrong's 60 Shop, Armstrong's NavalYard, Brown's West Hartlepool, North-East Marine. (Middlesbrough failed to turn up).

1918-08-05 *North East Marine 3 - Willington Foundry 0*
Played at Murton Colliery AFC.

1918-08-17 *Consett Celtic 3 - Scotswood Munition Ladies 3*
Women v Men match played at the Vicarage Field, Consett, in aid of the Consett and District Homecoming Fund.
Scorers: Agnes Craig, Maggie Jayne & M. Gatherall for Scotswood; McKinney (2), Nichol for Consett.

1918-08-26 *Palmers v North East Marine*
Scheduled to be played at Curlew Road, Jarrow.

1918-08-31 *Horners Dainty Dinahs 1 - Haggies South Shore Ladies 1*
Played at the Secondary School, Durham Road, Gateshead, in aid of the Gateshead War Pensions Special Relief Fund.

1918-08-31 *Blyth Spartans Ladies 3 - Angus Sandersons Ladies 0*
Played at Croft Park, Blyth.
scorer: Bella Reay (3)
Spartans (from): M King (capt.), N Fairless, H Weir, A Sample, M O'Brien, B Metcalf, A Allen, S Rhodes, B Reay, J Morgan, M Jayne, N Cock, N Scruffin.
Angus-Sandersons: M Scott, B Smith, M Miller, S Dickson, F Wilson, M Lowery, S Bell, E Foster, E Lowes (capt.), M Charlton, E Armstrong, reserves: E Rowley, S Gransbury.

1918-08-31 *Palmers Girls 4 - Foster, Blackett & Wilsons Girls 0*

1918-09-07 *Durham 3 - Northumberland 0*

Played at the Rockcliffe Ground, Monkseaton in aid of the local branch of the Comrades of the Great War.

Durham: Maggie Scott (Foster Blackett's, Hebburn), Bella Smith (Angus Sandersons and Wrekenton), Julia Turnbull (Birtley), Lizzie Form (Palmer's, Jarrow), Bella Carrott, (North-East Marine and Gateshead), Lizzie Sayers (Foster Blackett's, Hebburn), Lizzie Lowes (Angus Sanderson, Wrekenton), Winnie McKenna (Grangetown), Sarah Cornforth (Birtley and Pelton), Mary Lyons (Palmer's, Jarrow), Minnie Seed (Palmers and Sunderland), reserves: Lizzie Gibson (Jarrow), Catherine Egan (Hebburn), Alice Churcher (Birtley).

Northumberland: May Horne (Wallsend Slipway), Hilda Weygood (North-East Marine), Maggie Short (Wallsend Slipway), Bella Willis (A. W. & Co. 60 Shop and Prudhoe), Ethel Jackson (North-East Marine), Grace Battista (60 Shop, Scotswood), Flo Wallace (North-East Marine), Ethel Wallace (57 Shop, Newcastle), Bella Reay (Blyth Spartans), Violet Bryant and Lizzie McConnell (Wallsend Slipway), reserves: Mary Mulligan, Agnes McConnell, Lizzie Watson (Wallsend).

1918-09-07 *Brown's Munition Girls 2 - Horden Munition Girls 0*

Scorer: Nellie Kirk (2).

1918-09-14 *Blyth Spartans v Angus Sanderson*

Scheduled to be played at Stakeford

Spartans: M. King (capt.), M. Fairless, H. Wear, S. Rhodes, A. Sample, M. O'Brien, N. Cocks, A. Allen, B. Reay, M. Scruffam, L. Morgan; reserve: Mary Lane.

1918-09-21 *England 5 - Ireland 2*

Played at St James's Park, Newcastle, in aid of the Lord Mayor's Relief Fund. A 90 yards sprint, a tug-of-war and a penalty kick competition were also staged. The event was poorly attended, with only 2,000 spectators, and takings at the gates amounted to only £60. In view of this Newcastle United waived their fee for the hire of the ground.

Scorers: Lyons (3), McKenna, Kirk for England; Hall (2) for Ireland.

England: (the posted team was as follows, but two players did not turn up; Mary Lyons of Palmer's was one of the substitutes) Scott (Jarrow), Weygood (Wallsend), Jackson (Wallsend), Willis (Prudhoe, capt.), Cornforth (West Pelton), Carrot (Gateshead), Dorrian (Hartlepools), Kirk (Hartlepools), McKenna (South Bank), Seed (Sunderland), McConnell (Rose Hill).

Ireland: Fisher (Belfast), Walker (Belfast), Moffat (Belfast), Ridell (Belfast, capt.), Forsyth (Ewart's, Antrim), McEwan (Belfast), Martin (Enniskillen), McLatchie (Portadown), Hall (Lurgan), Knox (Ewarts), Dolan (Belfast).

1918-09-26 *Dorman, Long (Britannia) v Skinningrove*

Munitionettes' Cup R1 scheduled to be played at Samuelson's ground, West Lane in aid of Sailor Jack's Orphans.

1918-09-28 *Birtley Munition Girls 1 - Wallsend Slipway Munition Girls 1*

Played at Birtley.

1918-10-12 *Durham 0 - Northumberland 1*

Played at St James's Park.

Durham: Ada Wildman (Annfield Plain), Bella Smith (Close Works, Gateshead), Lizzie Gibson (Palmer's Jarrow), Lily Proud (Haggie Bros, Gateshead), Bella Carrot (NEM and Gateshead), Lizzie Sawyers (F. B. & W. Hebburn), Mary Dorrian (West Hartlepool), Nellie Kirk (West Hartlepool), Lizzie E Lowes (Angus Sanderson and Wrekenton), Mary Lyons (Palmer's, Hebburn), Minnie Seed (Palmer's and Sunderland.

Northumberland: Sarah Atkinson (N.U.T. Benwell), Grace Battista (A. W. & Co. 60 Shop, Newcastle), Nellie Fairless (Blyth Spartans), Bella Willis (A, W & Co 60 Shop and Prudhoe, capt.), Martha O'Brien (Blyth Spartans), Cissie Short (A. W. & Co. 58 Shop), Flo Wallace (Wallsend), Annie Allen, Bella Reay (Blyth Spartans), Ethel Wallace (A. W. & Co. 57 Shop), Jennie Morgan (Blyth Spartans).

1918-10-19 *Browns v Richardson & Westgarth XI (Middlesbrough)*

Played at the Victoria Ground, Hartlepool in aid of the Indigent Sick Society.

1918-11-02 *Teesside Munitionettes v Tyneside Munitionettes*

Played at the Victoria Ground, Stockton.

Teesside: Hawthorn (Richardson Westgarth, Middlesbrough), Farrell (South Bank), Dukes (Dorman, Long & Co., Middlesbrough), Stott (Brown's, West Hartlepool), Lodge (Darlington), Plummer (West Hartlepool), Dorrian, Kirk (Brown's, West Hartlepool), McKenna (Grangetown), McKinitrie (Richardson Westgarth, Middlesbrough), McQuire (Dorman, Long & Co., Middlesbrough)

Tyneside: Sarah Atkinson (Newcastle), Bella Smith (Gateshead), Lizzie Gibson (Hebburn), Bella Willis (Prudhoe), Lizzie Form (Jarrow), Lily Scott (Newcastle), Lizzie Taylor (Jarrow), Lizzie Lowes (Wrekenton), Bella Reay, Mary Lyons (Blyth Spartans), Minnie Seed (Sunderland).

1918-11-02 *Haggie Bros 0 - Armstrong Whitworth 58 Shop 3*

Munitionettes Cup R1, played at St. James's Park.

Scorers: Charlton, Leightley, Gallagher.

1918-11-02 *Darlington Rise Carr 8 - Richardson, Westgarth & Co. (Middlesbrough) 1*

Played at Darlington

Scorers: S. Hooper (3) for Rise Carr; A. Fentiman for Richardsons (report incomplete).

1918-11-09 *Dorman Long & Co. 0 - Richardson, Westgarth 0*

Munitionettes' Cup R2, played at Dorman, Long's ground, Linthorpe before 1,000 spectators in aid of Christmas Parcels for enlisted men from the two companies.

Dorman's: Hodge, Simmonds, Dukes, Smith, McKay, Williams, Dunn, Humphries, McQuire, Bower, Haines

Richardson's: Hawthorn, Allen, Glen, O'Neil, Clay, Goodman, Fentiman, Jefferson, Buck, McKinstrie, Joyce.

1918-11-16 *Dorman Long & Co. v Richardson, Westgarth*

Munitionettes' Cup R2 replay at Samuelson's ground, West Lane, Newport.

1918-11-16 *Palmers Munitions Girls 3 - Hood Haggies Girls 0*

1918-11-16 *Greys 5 - Black & Whites 1*

This was to have been the Munitionettes Cup R2 encounter between Armstrong Whitworths and Wallsend North-East Marine, however the latter only had two fit players due to the flu epidemic. As a sizeable crowd had turned up at St James's Park a nine-a-side exhibition match was staged with the assistance of members of other teams in the crowd.

Scorers: Hutchinson (Haggies) 2, Carrot (N.E.M) 2 and Potts (Haggies) for the Greys; Wallace (Armstrong Whitworths) for the Black & Whites.

1918-11-23 *Foster, Blackett & Wilson 2 - Glaholm & Robson 1*

Played at Ashbrooke before a very large crowd in aid of the "Our Day" fund.

1918-11-23 *Hood Haggies Girls 0 - Palmers Munitionettes 4*

Munitionettes' Cup R1 played at Wallsend.

1918-11-23 *Armstrong Whitworths 43 Shop 1 - Newcastle Motor Company 2*

Munitionettes' Cup R1 played at Durham.

Scorers: Minnie Brandon (2) for NMC, Doris Noddoms for Armstrong Whitworths.

1918-11-23 *ABP & Co (Stockton) v Smith's Dock*

Munitionettes' Cup R2 at the Victoria Ground, Stockton in aid of St. Dunstan's Hostel for Blinded Soldiers and Sailors. (this was ABP's first match in the tournament)

Smith's Dock: N. Wells, A. Farrell, L. Powell, F. McNeil, M. Powell, M. Wyllie, S. English, L. Page, P. Page, G. Reece, A. Leach; Reserves: K. Watts, A. Graham.

1918-11-23 *Haggies Girls (Gateshead) 1 - Dainty Dinahs (Chester-le-Street) 0*

Played at Jarrow in aid of the Sailors' Orphans Fund.

Scorer: Mary Potts.

1918-11-23 *Armstrong Whitworths 1 - Vickers, Barrow 0*

Played at St James's Park before 5,000 spectators in aid of the Armstrong Whitworth's Girls' Benevolent Fund, and to settle the championship between the two, each side having won one of the previous two encounters.

Scorer: Sarah Cornforth.

Armstrong's: A. Shaw, G. Battista (60 Shop), J. Turnbull (Birtley C.C.F.), R. Cole (50 Shop), B. Willis (60 Shop), N. Innes (58 Shop), L. Spedding (Aviation), E. Fairbairn (57 Shop), S. Cornforth (Birtley C.C.F.), E. Wallace (57 Shop), H. Ruddock (Naval Yard)

Vickers: J. Percival, L. Wagstaff, L. Michaelson, A. Fletcher, M. Holmes, D. Cookson, M Christian, S. McLellan, W. Bradley, L. Parton, M. Dickinson.

1918-11-30 *Foster, Blackett's (Hebburn) 4 - Dainty Dinahs (Chester-le-Street) 0*

Munitionettes' Cup R1 played at Murray Park, Stanley.

Scorers: Maggie Scott (3), Maggie Blake.

1918-12-14 *Tyneside Munitionettes 4 - Brown's (Hartlepool) 0*

Played at St James's Park in aid of the Y.W.C.A. (reported in the Newcastle newspapers as Tyneside v Hartlepool)

Scorers: Bella Reay (2), Mary Lyons (2).

Tyneside: Sarah Atkinson (N.U.T. South Benwell), Bella Smith (Close Works and Angus Sanderson), Catherine Egan (Foster, Blackett and Wilson, Hebburn), Bella Willis (Armstrong, Whitworth & Co. 60 Shop, capt.), Cissie Short (Armstrong, Whitworth & Co. 58 Shop), Martha Lothian (Armstrong, Whitworth & Co. 57 Shop), Lizzie Taylor (Palmers), Sarah Henderson (58 Shop), Bella Reay (Blyth Spartans), Mary Lyons (Palmers), Minnie Seed (Sunderland).

1918-12-21 *Palmer's v Teesside*

Scheduled to be played at the Victoria Ground, Stockton – not reported.

1918-12-26 *ABP & Co. v Dorman Long & Co.*

Munitionettes R3 tie, scheduled to be played at Linthorpe, in aid of the Serbian (Sandes-Haverfield) Comforts Fund.

Dorman's: Jennie Hodge, Norah Humphries, Emily Simmonds, Martha Wood, Grace Williams, Nellie Mackay, Ethel Haines, Annie Bowers, Maggie McGuire, Lily Dunne, Kitty Gainsby; reserves: Lily Smith, Beatrice Rowley, Emily Simpson.

1918-12-26 *Tyneside Munitionettes 3 - Whitehaven Munitionettes 0*

Played at St. James's Park before 18,000 spectators; this was the first defeat for the Whitehaven team whose previous record was played 25, won 23, drawn 2.

Scorers: Dorrian, McKenna, Lyons

Tyneside: Sarah Atkinson (N.U.T., South Benwell), Grace Battista (A. W. & Co.), Lizzie Gibson (Palmers), Bella Willis (A. W. & Co. and Prudhoe), Cissie Short (A. W. & Co.), Lizzie Form (Palmers), Mary Dorrian (Brown's West Hartlepool), Winnie McKenna (South Bank), Bella Reay (Blyth Spartans), Mary Lyons (Palmers), Minnie Seed (Sunderland).

Whitehaven: Kitty Cowie, May Elwood, Cissie Spedding, Ida Robinson, Winnie Whirity (capt.), Gladys Field, Elsie Lowes, Maggie Cunningham, Vera Wilson, Mary Milne.

1918-12-28 *Brown's 7 - Darlington Munitionettes 0*

Munitionettes R2 tie, played at Hartlepool.

1919-01-01 *Northumberland v Durham & North Yorks*

Scheduled for the Victoria Ground, Stockton on New Year's Day

Durham and North Yorks: Florrie Holmes (West Hartlepool), Amelia Farrell (South Bank), Lizzie Gibson (Hebburn), Nellie Stott (West Hartlepool), Lizzie Form (Jarrow), Annie Wharton (Eston), Mary Dorrian, Nellie Kirk (West Hartlepool), Winnie McKenna (Grangetown), Mary Lyons (Jarrow), Minnie Seed (Sunderland)

Northumberland: Sarah Atkinson (Newcastle), Grace Battista (Newcastle), Nellie Fairless (Blyth), Bella Willis (Prudhoe, capt.), Martha O'Brien (Blyth), Lily Scott (Newcastle), Beatrice Taylor (Newcastle), Sarah Henderson (Delaval), Bella Reay (Blyth), Ethel Wallace (Scotswood), Annie Allen (Blyth).

1919-01-02 *Teesside v Armstrongs*

Scheduled for the Victoria Ground, Stockton. Armstrongs intended to field Bella Reay.

1919-01-18 *Whitehaven Ladies 1 - Tyneside Ladies 1*

Played at Whitehaven before a crowd of 5-6,000.

scorers: Reay for Tyneside, Wilson for Whitehaven.

1919-02-01 *Brown's Girls 1 - Horden Girls 0*
Munitionettes Cup Quarter-Final
Brown's (from): Holmes, Cambridge, Knight, Hodgson, Snowball, Kelly, Booth, Henderson, Stott (capt.), Dorrian, Kirk, McKenna, McPherson, Ferguson.

1919-02-08 *Palmers Jarrow 4 - Armstrong Whitworth 1*
Munitionettes' Cup Quarter-Final played at St James's Park.
Scorer: Bella Reay (3).

1919-02-08 *Foster, Blackett & Wilson's 1 - Armstrong Whitworth (Scotswood) 0*
Munitionettes' Cup Quarter-Final played at Jarrow.
Scorer: Maggie Scott (Note: Scotswood had only 7 players).

1919-03-01 *Palmers (Jarrow and Hebburn) 3 - Foster, Blackett & Wilson's 2*
Munitionettes' Cup semi-final played on the Pit Heap Ground, Curlew Road, Jarrow.
Scorers: Scott, Wilson for Foster Blackett's, Taylor (pen), Seed, Hagan (o.g.) for Palmer's.

1919-03-08 *Dick, Kerr's (Preston) Girls 1 - Newcastle Girls 0*
Played at Deepdale (Preston North End) before 5,000 spectators, raising £179 for charity.
Newcastle: Sarah Atkinson, Catherine Egan, Lizzie Gibson, Bella Willis, Cissie Short, Lizzie Form, Mary Dorrian, Nellie Kirk, Winnie McKenna, Mary Lyons, Minnie Seed (Note: This was a North-East rather than a Newcastle team).

1919-03-15 *Brown's 2 - Teesside 0*
Played at Stockton.

1919-03-22 *Palmers (Jarrow and Hebburn) 1 - Browns (West Hartlepool 0)*
Munitionettes' Cup Final played at St James's Park before 9,000 spectators. Both teams included top-class players from other sides, as indicated below.
Scorer: Bella Reay
Palmers: L. Green, A. Malone, L. Gibson, B. Willis (Armstrong-Whitworth's), L. Form (capt.) E. Drinkeld, B. Taylor, E. Graham, B. Reay (Blyth Spartans), M. Lyons, M. Seed (Gosforth Aviation)
Brown's: F. Holmes, E. Cambridge, R. Knight, M. Hodgson, N. Henderson, N. Stott (capt.), M. Dorrian, N. Kirk, W. McKenna (Bolckow, Vaughan), M. McPherson, E. Ferguson .

1919-04-22 *Newcastle Girls 0 - Dick, Kerr's Girls (Preston) 0*

Played at St James's Park before 25-30,000 spectators.

Newcastle: Florrie Holmes, Grace Battista, Catherine Egan, Bella Willis (capt.), Martha O'Brien, Lizzie Form, Mary Dorrian, Winnie McKenna, Bella Reay, Mary Lyons, Minnie Seed.

Preston: Hastie, Hulme, Kell (capt.), Jones, Walmsley, Rawthorne, Redford, Partington, Harris, Standing, Walker.

1919-05-10 *Teesside Ladies 1 - Tyneside Ladies 1*

Played at Ayresome Park in aid of the YWCA before 2,000 spectators

Scorers: Beattie Taylor (Tyneside), Mary Lyons (Teesside)

Tyneside: Ada Shaw or Sarah Atkinson, Catherine Egan, Lizzie Gibson, Bella Willis, Cissie Short, Lizzie Form, Beattie Taylor, Elsie Graham, Bella Reay, Mary Lyons, Lizzie McConnell, reserves - Lily Scott, Violet Bryant

Teesside: Florrie Holmes, Grace Battista, Harriet Knight, Bella Henderson, Bella Plummer, Annie Wharton, Mary Dorrian, Nellie Kirk, Winnie McKenna (capt.), Mabel McKinskie, Minnie Seed, reserves - Jennie Hodge, Amelia Farrell, Maggie McGuire, Lily Dunn.

1919-05-17 *Brown's 1 - Palmers (Hebburn & Jarrow) 3*

Played at West Hartlepool.

Scorers: Beattie Taylor, Elsie Graham (2) for Palmers, Mary Dorrian for Brown's

(Willis captained Palmer's).

1919-05-24 *Sunderland Munitionettes 1 - Newcastle Munitionettes 4*

Played at Roker Park before 10,000 spectators, raising £436 for the Haverfield Serbian Distress Fund.

Scorers: Lyons (3), McGuire for Newcastle, Kirk for Sunderland

Sunderland: Holmes, Cambridge, Knight, Henderson, Plummer, Drinkeld, Dorrian, Kirk, McKenna, Seed (capt.) , McConnell

Newcastle: Atkinson, Egan, Gibson, Willis (capt.), Short, Form, Taylor, Baine, McGuire, Lyons, Graham.

1919-05-31 *Newcastle Munitionettes 4 - Sunderland Munitionettes 0*

Played at St James's Park before 9,000 spectators in aid of the Newcastle (Central) Division of the St John's Ambulance Brigade.

Scorers: Taylor (3 - 1 pen), Lyons.

Newcastle: Atkinson, Egan, Gibson, Willis (capt.), Short, Form, Taylor, Graham, McGuire, Lyons, Bains

Sunderland: Holmes (West Hartlepool), Battista, Knight, Henderson, O'Brien (Blyth Spartans), Plummer, Dorrian (West Hartlepool), McKenna (South Bank), Reay (Blyth Spartans) or Kirk, Seed (capt.), McConnell

Appendix 2

Munitionette Players

This is an alphabetical list of 485 players whose names appear in newspaper reports of munitionette football matches. The list has been edited to correct obvious spelling errors. Some of the entries may be duplicates, where the full name has appeared in one report but only the initial in another.

Abbey, Becca	Expanded Metal Co.
Adams, J.	Dorman, Long & Co.
Adamson, M.	Glaholm & Robson
Agar, Harriet	Expanded Metal Co.
Aitken, N.	North East Marine
Allan or Allen, Annie	Blyth Spartans
Allan or Allen, Dollie	Blyth Spartans
Allan, Hilda	CMEW
Allen, E.	Richardson Westgarth
Anderson, S	Glaholm & Robson
Andrews, Ettie	Armstrong 57 Shop
Appleton, Mary	Rise Carr
Arkless, Jane	Birtley CCF
Armstrong, A.	Armstrong 58 Shop
Armstrong, E.	Angus Sanderson
Armstrong, S.	Glaholm & Robson
Arthur, Isabella	Wallsend Slipway
Ashton, Emily	Rise Carr
Atkin, Mary	North East Marine
Atkinson B.	Sunderland Ladies
Atkinson, Mary	Expanded Metal Co.
Atkinson, Sarah	N.U.T. South Benwell
Atkinson, S.	Blyth United
Atlass, M.	Birtley Shell Shop

Bailey, L.	Richardson Westgarth
Bainbridge, N.	Palmer's
Balls, J.	Blyth United
Barnett, M.	Richardson Westgarth
Barnett, Norah	Expanded Metal Co.
Battista, Grace	Armstrong 60 Shop
Beatty, E.	Webster & Co.
Bell, S.	Angus Sanderson
Belton, N.	Birtley Shell Shop
Benson, Florence	Gosforth Aviation
Best, Maud	Gosforth Aviation
Biddle, M.	Sacriston Ladies
Blake, Maggie	Foster Blackett
Blake, M.	Hood, Haggie's
Blewett, H.	Rise Carr
Bolland, E.	Hood, Haggie's
Booth, Matilda	Christopher Brown Ltd
Bowers, Annie	Dorman, Long & Co.
Bowie, A.	Armstrong 60 Shop
Boyle, R.	Dorman's Port Clarence
Brandon, Minnie	Newcastle Motor Co.
Briggs, A.	Dorman's Port Clarence
Brittan, A.	Rise Carr
Brown, J	Ashmore, Benson, Pease
Brown, M.	Morpeth Post Office
Bruce, M.	North East Marine
Bryant, Violet	Wallsend Slipway
Buckley, A.	Glaholm & Robson
Buddington, M.	Webster & Co.
Burke, M.	Blyth United
Burns, J.	CMEW

Cairns, D.	Morpeth Post Office
Cambridge, E.	Christopher Brown Ltd
Campbell, Mabel	CMEW
Cappelman, B.	Armstrong 57 Shop
Carnaby, H.	Blyth Spartans
Carr, K.	Armstrong 57 Shop
Carr, L.	Angus Sanderson
Carr, Maggie	Gosforth Aviation
Carrott, Bella	North East Marine
Catchesides, F.	Sunderland Ladies
Catterick, Edith (Ettie)	North East Marine
Cavanagh, Susan	CMEW
Chambers, Grace	Wallsend Slipway
Chapman, E.	Birtley Shell Shop
Charlton, A.	Armstrong 58 Shop
Charlton, M.	Angus Sanderson
Charlton, H.	Armstrong 58 Shop
Churcher, Alice	Birtley CCF
Clark, Elizabeth	Wallsend Slipway
Clark, S.	Hood, Haggie's
Clarke, N.	Birtley CCF
Clay, J.	Dorman's Port Clarence
Cock, N.	Blyth Spartans
Cole, Isabella (Bella)	Armstrong 57 Shop
Cole, Bessie	Armstrong 57 Shop
Cole, R.	Armstrong 60 Shop
Connell, J.	Burradon Ladies
Connelly, Dolly	Gosforth Aviation
Cooke, E.	Hood, Haggie's
Cooper, Maggie	Armstrong 60 Shop
Cornforth, Sarah	Birtley CCF
Connon, Christiana	Palmer's
Connon, Susannah	Palmer's
Conway, C.	Smith's Dock
Cowie, Kitty	Whitehaven
Craig, Agnes	Armstrong Whitworth

Craig, A.	Hood, Haggie's
Crier, E.	Bolckow, Vaughan
Crone, L.	Sunderland Ladies
Crosby, J.	Sunderland Ladies
Cunningham, Maggie	Whitehaven
Curry, Mary	Foggins 43 Shop
Cusworth, Ada	Christopher Brown Ltd
Davidson, E.	Webster & Co.
Davis, J.	Ashmore, Benson, Pease
Davison, E.	Blyth United
Day, F.	Glaholm & Robson
Dearden, F.	Hood, Haggie's
Denny, A.	Richardson Westgarth
Dent, L.	Birtley Shell Shop
Dickinson, Jessie	Armstrong 60 Shop
Dickson, S.	Angus Sanderson
Dingnall, C.	Sunderland Ladies
Dodds, C.	Glaholm & Robson
Dodds, F.	Ashmore, Benson, Pease
Doeck, M.	North East Marine
Donkin, I.	Webster & Co.
Donnelly, L.	Dorman's Port Clarence
Donnelly, M.	Palmer's
Dorrian, Mary	Christopher Brown Ltd
Downey, M.	Blyth United
Drennan, G.	Richardson Westgarth
Drennan, M.	Birtley Shell Shop
Drinkald, E.	Armstrong 58 Shop
Drinkeld, E.	Palmer's
Dryden, M	Armstrong 43 Shop
Duff, J.	Hood, Haggie's
Dukes, A.	Dorman, Long & Co.
Dunn, Lilian or Lily	Dorman, Long & Co.
Earley, E.	Birtley CCF
Edwards, L.	Smith's Dock

Egan, Catherine	Foster Blackett
Elwood, May	Whitehaven
English, N.	Sunderland Ladies
English, Sarah	Smith's Dock
Evis, M.	Ashmore, Benson, Pease
Ewen, S.	Sacriston Ladies
Fairbairn, Ella	Armstrong 57 Shop
Fairless, Nellie	Blyth Spartans
Fannen, A.	Hood, Haggie's
Farrell, Amelia	Bolckow, Vaughan
Fawcus, A.	Palmer's
Fentiman, A.	Richardson Westgarth
Ferguson, E.	Christopher Brown Ltd
Fewster, N.	Dorman's Port Clarence
Field, Gladys	Whitehaven
Finlay, Lizzie	Birtley CCF
Fleck, May	Wallsend Slipway
Floyd, A.	Bolckow, Vaughan
Form, Lizzie	Palmer's
Foster, D.	Carlisle
Foster, E.	Angus Sanderson
Foster, M.	Blyth United
Fox, S.	Glaholm & Robson
Gainsby, Kitty	Dorman, Long & Co.
Gallagher, F.	Armstrong 58 Shop
Gallagher, Lizzie	Armstrong 60 Shop
Gallagher, L.	Dorman's Port Clarence
Gardner, Elsie	Armstrong 60 Shop
Gascoine, M.	Birtley CCF
Gatherall, M.	Armstrong Whitworth
Gatherer, M. A.	Hood, Haggie's
Gibson, Lizzie	Palmer's

Gillespie, S.	Blyth United
Glancey, M.	Ashmore, Benson, Pease
Glass, M.	Armstrong 58 Shop
Goodman, G.	Richardson Westgarth
Gould, Laura	Armstrong 57 Shop
Graham, A.	Smith's Dock
Graham, Elsie	Palmer's
Gransbury, S.	Angus Sanderson
Gray, May	Wallsend Slipway
Green, Lizzie	Palmer's
Greig, E.	Hood, Haggie's
Grey, A.	Sunderland Ladies
Griffiths, Violet	CMEW

Haines, Ethel	Dorman, Long & Co.
Hall, E.	Ashmore, Benson, Pease
Halliday, B.	Webster & Co.
Hamilton, N.	Christopher Brown Ltd
Harding, Eva	Wallsend Slipway
Hardman, A.	Dorman's Port Clarence
Hardy, S.	Sunderland Ladies
Harris, Florrie	Blyth Spartans
Hartley, A.	Smith's Dock
Harvey, Agnes	CMEW
Harvey, H.	Blyth Spartans
Hawkes, E.	Rise Carr
Hawthorne, G.	Richardson Westgarth
Hayton, Margaret	Wallsend Slipway
Henderson, Bella	Teesside
Henderson, E.	CMEW
Henderson, E.	Angus Sanderson
Henderson, N.	Christopher Brown Ltd
Henderson, Sarah	Armstrong 58 Shop
Hendry, G.	Armstrong 60 Shop
Henry, A.	Morpeth Post Office
Herd, E.	Christopher Brown Ltd
Herdman, L.	Birtley CCF

Heron, N.	Walker Naval Yard
Hicks, Emma	Morpeth Post Office
Hill, A.	Walker Naval Yard
Hindmarsh, S.	Morpeth Post Office
Hinson, Alice	Armstrong 60 Shop
Hipkin, A.	Armstrong 57 Shop
Hodge, Jennie	Dorman, Long & Co.
Hodgson, M.	Christopher Brown Ltd
Holloran, Bridget	North East Marine
Holmes, Florrie	Christopher Brown Ltd
Hooper, Sarah	Rise Carr
Hooton, G.	Glaholm & Robson
Horne, May	Wallsend Slipway
Humphries, Norah	Dorman, Long & Co.
Innes, N.	Armstrong 57 Shop
Ions, Gertie	Armstrong 60 Shop
Irving, Charlotte	Armstrong 60 Shop
Irwin, Emily	Gosforth Aviation
Irwin, Sarah	Birtley CCF
Jackson, Ethel	North East Marine
James, Lizzie	Blyth Spartans
Jameson, M.	Armstrong 58 Shop
Jayne, M.	Blyth Spartans
Jayne, Maggie	Armstrong Whitworth
Jefferson, Gertie	Richardson, Westgarth
Jennings, T.	Armstrong 58 Shop
Johnson, E.	Gosforth Aviation
Johnson, L.	Rise Carr
Johnson, N.	Walker Naval Yard
Jones, G.	Armstrong 60 Shop
Kane, Lizzie	Expanded Metal Co.
Keen, A.	Birtley Shell Shop

Kelly, P.	Morpeth Post Office
Kelley, G.	Christopher Brown Ltd
Kennedy, N.	Birtley CCF
Kidney, Alice	Webster & Co.
King, Amy	CMEW
King, M.	Blyth Spartans
Kirk, Greta	Bolckow, Vaughan
Knight, Harriet	Teesside
Koltz, Mary	Sunderland Ladies
Lacey, Blanche	Wallsend Slipway
Lambeth, F.	Sacriston Ladies
Lane, Mary	Blyth Spartans
Laverick, L.	Birtley Shell Shop
Lawrence, L.	Dorman's Port Clarence
Lawson, V.	Webster & Co.
Lawton, H.	Blyth United
Leach, A.	Bolckow, Vaughan
Leach, M.	Gosforth Aviation
Leggett, R.	Trimdon Grange
Leighton, Jennie	CMEW
Leighton, J.	Armstrong 58 Shop
Leobie, G.	Burradon Ladies
Liddle, M.	Birtley CCF
Lincoln, G.	Glaholm & Robson
Lister, Frances	Armstrong 60 Shop
Lister, L.	Walker Naval Yard
Little, D.	Birtley Shell Shop
Littlefair, J.	Burradon Ladies
Lodge, Jessie	Rise Carr
Lonsdale, Nellie	Birtley Shell Shop
Lothian, Martha	Armstrong 57 Shop
Lowcock, Doris	CMEW
Lowery, Lizzie	Blyth Spartans
Lowes, Elsie	Whitehaven
Lowes, M.	Morpeth Post Office
Lowry, M.	Angus Sanderson

Lowson, V.	Webster & Co.
Lyons, Mary	Palmer's
Lythe, D.	Rise Carr
Macaulay, L	Palmer's
Mackay, Nellie	Dorman, Long & Co.
Mahon, N.	Bolckow, Vaughan
Malabar, M.	Birtley CCF
Mallon, A.	Hood, Haggie's
Malone, Hannah	Blyth Spartans
Malone, M.	Burradon Ladies
Mansfield, Sylvia	Gosforth Aviation
March, Lizzie	Christopher Brown Ltd
Marsh, J.	Birtley CCF
Marsh, L.	Birtley CCF
Martin, J.	Bolckow, Vaughan
Martin, V.	Bolckow, Vaughan
McBride, S.	Sunderland Ladies
McCann, C.	North East Marine
Matthews, Sally	Birtley CCF
McCarron, Annie	North East Marine
McConnell, Agnes	Wallsend Slipway
McConnell, Elizabeth	Wallsend Slipway
McCormack, S.	Sunderland Ladies
McCormick, Sarah	Sunderland Ladies
McCulley/McNully, A.	Webster & Co.
McCulley/McNully, M.	Webster & Co.
McGregor, Mary	Wallsend Slipway
McGuigan, L.	Rise Carr
McGuire, Maggie	Dorman, Long & Co.
McIntyre, A.	Dorman's Port Clarence
McKay, E.	Workington
McKay, M.	Morpeth Post Office
McKenna, Winnie	Bolckow, Vaughan
McKenzie, M.	Christopher Brown Ltd
McKinstry, Mabel	Dorman, Long & Co.

McNeil, F.	Smith's Dock
McPherson, M.	Christopher Brown Ltd
Meadows, M.	Walker Naval Yard
Metcalfe, Bella	Blyth Spartans
Middleton, N.	Birtley CCF
Miller, M.	Angus Sanderson
Milne, Mary	Whitehaven
Milner, Emily	Bolckow, Vaughan
Mitchell, L.	Birtley Shell Shop
Moffat, E.	Sacriston Ladies
Mohan, Mary	Bolckow, Vaughan
Moon, W.	Webster & Co.
Mordey, C.	Glaholm & Robson
Mordue, H.	Sacriston Ladies
Morgan, Jane (Jennie)	Blyth Spartans
Mulligan, Mary	Wallsend Slipway
Murdock, Nance	Armstrong 60 Shop
Murphy, R.	Bolckow, Vaughan
Murray, E.	Webster & Co.
Murray, Norah	Christopher Brown Ltd
Neison, N.	Armstrong 60 Shop
Nelson, A.	North East Marine
Nendick, L.	Walker Naval Yard
Nistram, N.	Richardson Westgarth
Noble, H.	Sunderland Ladies
Noddons, Doris	Armstrong 43 Shop
Norris, Florrie	CMEW
North, G.	Burradon Ladies
Nuttall, Jane (Jennie)	Blyth Spartans
O'Brien, Martha	Blyth Spartans
O'Connell, M.	Richardson Westgarth
O'Donnell, K.	Sunderland Ladies
Ormston, E.	Angus Sanderson

Page, L.	Smith's Dock
Page, Mercy	Bolckow, Vaughan
Park, A.	Rise Carr
Parker, J.	Glaholm & Robson
Patterson, S.	Glaholm & Robson
Pearson, M.	Birtley Shell Shop
Pease, L.	Burradon Ladies
Percival, Olive	Bolckow, Vaughan
Phillips, K.	Angus Sanderson
Plummer, Bella	Expanded Metal Co.
Porthouse, M.	Palmer's
Potts, B.	Richardson Westgarth
Potts, J.	Morpeth Post Office
Potts, Mary	Haggie's, Gateshead
Price, A.	Birtley CCF
Proud, Lily	Haggie's, Gateshead
Powell, Elizabeth	Bolckow, Vaughan
Powell, M.	Smith's Dock
Quigley, B.	Richardson Westgarth's
Quinn, M.	Wallsend Slipway
Raine, S.	Carlisle
Ramshaw, Elizabeth	Armstrong 60 Shop
Reay, Isabella (Bella)	Blyth Spartans
Reed, Ada	Blyth Spartans
Reed, M.	Sunderland Ladies
Reece, Gladys	Bolckow, Vaughan
Relton, Annie	Expanded Metal Co.
Relton, Mary	Expanded Metal Co.
Rhodes, S.	Blyth Spartans
Richmond, H.	Sunderland Ladies

Ridley, K.	Ashmore, Benson, Pease
Ritchie, E.	Ashmore, Benson, Pease
Rix, R.	Hood, Haggie's
Roberts, L.	Rise Carr
Robertson, N.	Palmer's
Robinson, Ida	Whitehaven
Robinson, M.	Dorman's Port Clarence
Robson, E.	Hood, Haggie's
Robson, L.	Dorman's Port Clarence
Rodgers, B.	Webster & Co.
Rothwell, Florrie	North East Marine
Rowans, M	Hood, Haggie's
Rowell, A.	Bolckow, Vaughan
Rowley, Beatrice	Dorman, Long & Co.
Rowley, E.	Angus Sanderson
Ruddock, Hilda	Walker Naval Yard
Russell, Jenny	Armstrong 60 Shop
Russell, M.	Webster & Co.
Rutter, Maud	CMEW
Sample, Agnes	Blyth Spartans
Sanderson, E.	Webster & Co.
Saunders, E.	Hood, Haggie's
Sayers/Sawyers, Lizzie	Foster, Blackett
Scott, E.	North East Marine
Scott, Maggie	Palmer's/Foster Blackett
Scott, M.	Glaholm & Robson
Scruffin, N.	Blyth Spartans
Scullion, S.	Rise Carr
Seal, May	CMEW
Seed, Minnie	Aviation / Naval Yard
Sharples, Violet	Bolckow, Vaughan
Shaw, Ada	Armstrong 60 Shop
Sherry, Theresa	Belle Vue
Shields, M.	Blyth United
Short, Cissie	Armstrong 58 Shop
Short, Maggie	Wallsend Slipway

Simmonds, Emily	Dorman, Long & Co.
Simms, Ada	Gosforth Aviation
Simpson, Emily	Dorman, Long & Co.
Smith, Amy	Sunderland Ladies
Smith, Bella	Angus Sanderson
Smith, Lily	Dorman, Long & Co.
Smith, M.	Blyth United
Smith, Nellie	CMEW
Smith, O.	Richardson Westgarth
Snowball, E.	Christopher Brown Ltd
Spedding, Cissie	Whitehaven
Spedding, Lizzie	Gosforth Aviation
Spenceley, Jessie	Expanded Metal Co.
Spinks, M.	Blyth United
Steel, J.	Gosforth Aviation
Stevenson, Edie	Expanded Metal Co.
Stevenson, Margaret	Wallsend Slipway
Stevenson, Martha	Expanded Metal Co.
Stewart, H.	Palmer's
Stockdale, F.	Sacriston Ladies
Storey, E.	Hood, Haggie's
Storey, M.	Sacriston Ladies
Stott, Nellie	Christopher Brown Ltd
Summers, Dollie	Blyth Spartans
Taylor, A.	Dorman's Port Clarence
Taylor, Beattie	Palmer's
Taylor, Florence	Armstrong 60 Shop
Taylor, H.	Dorman's Port Clarence
Templeman, Annie	Ashmore, Benson, Pease
Thomas, E.	Ashmore, Benson, Pease
Thompson, Bella	Walker Naval Yard
Thompson, E.	Sacriston Ladies
Thompson, F.	Blyth United
Thompson, Maggie	Wallsend Slipway
Thwaites, A.	Glaholm & Robson
Timbers, G.	Wallsend Slipway

Tingley, N.	Sunderland Ladies
Todd, J.	Ashmore, Benson, Pease
Todd, M.	Palmer's
Tomlinson, M.	Webster & Co.
Trueman, Violet	Ashmore, Benson, Pease
Tuck, E.	Hood, Haggie's
Turnbull, Bella	Wallsend Slipway
Turnbull, Julia	Birtley CCF
Turner, Dollie	Blyth Spartans
Tweddle, Florence	Gosforth Aviation
Tyson, L.	CMEW
Vinckley, M.	Dorman, Long & Co.
Wade, M.	Morpeth Post Office
Walker, H.	Sunderland Ladies
Wallace, Ethel	Armstrong 57 Shop
Wallace, Florrie	North East Marine
Wardaugh, Ina	Walker Naval Yard
Waters, Emma	Gosforth Aviation
Watson, A.	Armstrong 57 Shop
Watson, C.	Hood, Haggie's
Watson, Jane	Wallsend Slipway
Watson, J.	Blyth United
Watson, M.	Webster & Co.
Watson, M.	Walker Naval Yard
Watts, K.	Smith's Dock
Weightman, Kitty	Palmer's
Weir, Hannah	Blyth Spartans
Wells, E.	Smith's Dock
Wells, R.	Smith's Dock
West, A.	Morpeth Post Office
Wharton, Annie	Bolckow, Vaughan
Whirity, Winnie	Whitehaven
White, A.	Dorman's Port Clarence

Whiteside, S.	Glaholm & Robson
Wildman, Ada	Armstrong 43 Shop
Wilkinson, Mary	CMEW
Williams, Grace	Dorman, Long & Co.
Williams, L.	Hood, Haggie's
Willis, Bella	Armstrong 60 Shop
Wilson, F.	Angus Sanderson
Wilson, F.	North East Marine
Wilson, Sarah S.	Sunderland Ladies
Wilson, Vera	Whitehaven
Wood, M.	Morpeth Post Office
Wood, Martha	Dorman, Long & Co.
Wooton, Grace	Glaholm & Robson
Wright, J.	Glaholm & Robson
Wyley, M.	Smith's Dock
Wynn, Elizabeth	Armstrong 60 Shop
Yeaman, A.	Wallsend Slipway
Young, A.	Glaholm & Robson
Young, Ethel	Gosforth Aviation
Young, Elizabeth	Palmer's

Appendix 3

North-East Munitions Companies

Angus, Sanderson & Co. Ltd
Motor manufacturer, situated at St Thomas's Street, Newcastle,

Armstrong, Whitworth & Co.
A major manufacturer of ships and armaments, with shipyards at Elswick and Walker, arms factories at Elswick, Scotswood and Birtley, and aircraft assembly at Grandstand Road, Gosforth.

Ashmore, Benson, Pease & Co.
Foundry and engineering works - based in Stockton,

Bolckow, Vaughan & Co.
Steel manufacturers and converters, with premises at Eston and Middlesbrough.

Cartridge Case Factory, Birtley
(see Armstrong, Whitworth)

Central Marine Engine Works
Marine engine department of Gray's Shipyard, situated at Central Road, Hartlepool. Part of the site was given over to shell manufacture.

Christopher Brown Ltd
Saw mills - based in Stranton, West Hartlepool.

Craven and Speeding
Manufacturer of rope, based in Sunderland.

Dorman, Long & Co.
Steel manufacturers and converters, with premises at Port Clarence and South Bank, Teesside.

Foster, Blackett & Wilson Ltd
Manufacturers of lead and lead-based pigments, situated in Blackett Street, Jarrow. During the Great War the company manufactured shrapnel.

Glaholm, Robson & Co.
Manufacturer of wire rope, situated at 55 Hendon Road, Sunderland.

Gosforth Aviation
(see Armstrong, Whitworth)

Naval Yard, Walker
(see Armstrong, Whitworth)

North Eastern Marine Engineering Company
Ship builders, situated at Wallsend and Sunderland.

North Eastern Railway

The North Eastern Railway had engineering workshops at Darlington which included a shell manufacturing shop, owned by Armstrong-Whitworth but managed on their behalf by the NER.

NUT Motor Company

Manufacturer of motorcycles, situated in South Benwell Road, South Benwell, Newcastle.

Palmer's Shipbuilding and Iron Company Ltd

Iron smelter and shipbuilder, situated in Western Road, Jarrow.

Richardson, Westgarth & Co.

Manufacturer of marine engines, with premises at Hartlepool (Thomas Richardson & Sons) and Middlesbrough (Sir Christopher Furness, Westgarth and Co.)

Ridley's (Skinningrove) Ltd

Situated at Skinningrove, near Redcar.

Rise Carr Rolling Mills

Manufacturer of steel railway lines, situated at Rise Carr, Darlington.

Robert Hood Haggie & Son Ltd

Manufacturers of hempen and wire ropes, with premises at Willington Quay and Redheugh, Gateshead.

Robert Stephenson & Co.

Manufacturer of railway engines, situated at Springfield, Darlington.

Skinningrove Ironworks

Situated at Skinningrove, near Redcar.

Smith's Dock

Ship repairers, situated at South Bank, Teesside.

The Expanded Metal Company

Manufacturers of expanded metal mesh, situated in West Hartlepool.

Wallsend Slipway and Engineering Company

Ship repairers and manufacturers of marine boilers and engines, situated at Wallsend-on-Tyne.

Webster & Co.

Manufacturer of rope, situated at 4, Ropery Walk, Deptford, Sunderland.